"Your Loving Son":

Letters of an RCAF Navigator

"Your Loving Son":

Letters of an RCAF Navigator

edited by Stephen L.V. King

Canadian Plains Research Center, 2002

UNIVERSITY OF
REGINA

Canadian Plains Research Center
University of Regina
Regina, Saskatchewan S4S 0A2 Canada
Tel: (306) 585-4758
Fax: (306) 585-4699
e-mail: canadian.plains@uregina.ca
http://www.cprc.ca

National Library of Canada Cataloguing in Publication

King, George McCowan, 1922–1943
"Your loving son": letters of an RCAF navigator/[George McCowan King]; Stephen L.V. King, editor.

(Canadian plains studies, ISSN 0317-6290 ; 41)
Includes bibliographical references.
ISBN 0-88977-149-9

1. King, George McCowan, 1922–1943. 2. World War, 1939–1945—Aerial operations, Canadian.
3. World War, 1939–1945—Saskatchewan. 4. Canada. Royal Canadian Air Force—Biography.
5. Flight navigators—Canada—Biography. I. King, Stephen L.V. (Stephen Leslie Val), 1972–
II. University of Regina. Canadian Plains Research Center. III. Title. IV. Series.
D811.K563 2002   940.54'4971'092   C2002-911220-6

Cover Design: Brian Danchuk Design

Printed and bound in Canada by Houghton Boston, Saskatoon, Saskatchewan

Printed on acid-free paper

To George and James:

"Oft in the stilly night,
Ere slumber's chain has bound me,
Fond Memory brings the light
Of other days around me."

Thomas Moore, "The Light of Other Days"

Table of Contents

Acknowledgements

Many people helped me as I completed this book, and I owe them all a great debt.

Bob Cole and Dan Duda encouraged me to undertake the project, and it is due largely to their interest that I was able to maintain the focus needed to complete it. Ken Tingley provided me with sound guidance at the outset, and Jonathan Meakin has remained supportive over the past few years.

As usual, Dr Rick Bowers has been a great help. He provided me with invaluable advice as I began to search for a publisher, and his enthusiasm has been an inspiration throughout the writing process.

I have two reasons to thank Neil Erickson: for the interest he has shown in the project for the past few years, and for the map he drew by hand which appears on page 15.

I would like to thank the staff at the Canadian Plains Research Center, particularly Donna Achtzehner and Brian Mlazgar, for their belief in the project and their editorial assistance as the book neared completion. I must also thank Gerry Hill and Doug Chisholm for the inspiration that their own work has provided.

The members of my extended family have been very supportive as I have worked on the book. Gail and Crista Bradley have always shown a tremendous amount of interest in my work, and Doreen Hobson has provided me with a wealth of information about the Summerberry and Grenfell districts. Mike Binns, Bruce Dawson, and Sophie Grahame have provided valuable friendship over the course of my work, and Ann and Philip Grahame helped paint a vivid picture for me of life in wartime England.

I am very grateful to my immediate family. I could not have completed this work without Cara Bradley. For many years, she has been a source of love and encouragement, and her research skills have often enabled me to track down necessary pieces of information. My mother, Claire, has demonstrated great enthusiasm for the project, and has proven very helpful in identifying people mentioned in the letters. My brother Ross has found valuable information in England that would otherwise have been unavailable to me. Other of my siblings have been equally supportive. Randy, Karen, Maureen, and Wendy have been willing audiences for early drafts of the work, and have shown a great deal of interest in the project throughout. My cousin George King helped me to delineate my family history and to identify many of the individuals named in the book

Most of all, I must thank my late father, James. His love for a brother who died too young infuses this book, and his fond remembrances of a youth spent in Summerberry gave me the means to complete it.

ROYAL CANADIAN AIR FORC

CHAPLAIN SERVICES

R.C

Nov

Mr. W. King,
SUMMERBERRY, Sask.

Dear Mr. King:

You will no doubt have received the news that y
missing on the 22nd of September, is now believed to have been killed in action.

I know the sorrow that will prevail in you hearts on the receipt of
this news and I am deeply sympathetic. It does seem so final doesn't it and ends
the hope that would exist in your minds that your son might still be alive. I was
hoping too that the next letter I would write to you would be to join with you in
thanksgiving that George had turned up somewhere safe and sound, but evidently it
wasn't to be.

I had an Airmail from his Aunt, Mrs. McCowan, enquiring about him and
asking for more particulars. Unfortunately I have no more information than has been
relayed to you and I am quite sure if the casualty branch had anything to offer
further, they would do so. I knew George's Aunt, Mrs. McCowan when I was at Yorkton
as I had the unfortunate task of burying her boy when he was killed there. Would you
be good enough to pass on the word to her that I received her letter and that there
is nothing to add to what you already know.

I do pray that God will give you His strength at this time to bear
this tragic burden and keep alive in you heart a burning hope for the future, for
there is a future, whether it be here or hereafter God will vindicate His own word
and make all things, even the bitter things, work together for good. May there be
given to you and yours the comfort and the assurance that comes from His own word
in this matter.

One thing is worth holding on to and that is that George belongs now
to a great company who have enriched the world by their magnificent sacrifice. Free
people everywhere, lifted out of their bondage and suffering, must thank God for boys
like yours who have given all they had, to purchase that freedom. The price is heavy
we know, and will be heavier yet, but I know none who pay it more cheerfully than these
very fine boys over here. Its an inspiration to watch them and I can say quite truthfully there are none that I know of who would want to get out of it. Whatever happens
to them I don't know, but they seem to be lifted above desire for personal safety and
go on with the job, that has to be done with a quiet courageous efficiency that is
astounding. I went through the last war and I haven't seen anything like it. Its a
pity that such fine lads have to give their lives but you may be sure that while they
live they live, packing into a few short years experiences that are rich and full.

I do pray that you will not sorrow as those without hope and that in
the days that are to come you will have reason to be quietly proud in your own heart
that you had such a son and that you had such a cause to give him to.

Yours very sincerely,

W. Bell sh

Introduction:

"This Tragic Burden"

1

On the night of 22–23 September 1943, RAF Stirling Mk. III heavy bomber EF 139 left from Downham Market, England, as part of a mass bombing raid on Hannover, Germany. After dropping its ordnance over Hannover, the aircraft was hit by enemy fire, whereupon it exploded in mid-air and crashed near the town of Pohle, Germany. Two crewmen were able to parachute to relative safety: Air Gunner William Baker and Flight Engineer William Morement, though badly injured, were taken prisoner of war. The five other members of the crew— Pilot Norman Spencer, Bomb Aimer Douglas Wylie, Wireless Operator Harold Hicks, Mid-Upper Gunner Raymond Eberle, and Navigator George King—were unable to escape from the aircraft and were killed on impact.

Flight Sergeant George McCowan King.

Although this tragic event occurred almost thirty years before I was born, it has resonated with me all my life, for the navigator of that aircraft was my twenty-one-year-old uncle, RCAF Flight Sergeant George McCowan King. The pall which my uncle's death cast over those who had known him was an all-encompassing one. In his small hometown of Summerberry, Saskatchewan, he left behind many grieving friends, and of course his family, including my aged grandparents whose poor health left them ill-prepared to cope with the death of their youngest child. In addition, George left behind a number of relatives whom he had only recently met in England, and a brother who by being stationed in Atlantic Canada was situated between two worlds—the devastated one at home and the devastating one of the European theatre of war. The grief which my family experienced after George's death has been a longstanding one, since for the last six decades it was not only shared by his immediate family, but also passed on to me and my siblings through my father's memories of a younger brother whose life was tragically cut short in 1943.

From the time I was a young boy, George was a sort of absent presence in my life, for through the reminiscences of my father I felt that in some small way I had gotten to know an uncle who was destined never to know me. Only after I inherited his letters upon my father's death in 1991, however, did my uncle begin to become a truly human figure to me. Upon reading George's letters—letters that until her death in 1974 my grandmother lovingly kept bundled together by a yellow ribbon in a box along with a lock of his hair—I heard his irreverent but compassionate voice, experienced his lively personality, and felt his very real presence. Only then did I realise the severity of my family's loss and begin to understand what my father must have felt when he marched to the local cenotaph every Remembrance Day. I began to understand the pain felt by grandparents whom I never knew, but who as the recipients and preservers of these letters became silent partners with me as I sought to recover some sliver of this sad chapter in my family's history. And perhaps most importantly, I began to comprehend the great loss experienced by thousands of Canadian families who gave their beloved children in defence of our country.

When George King enlisted in the RCAF in the fall of 1941, he was not the first member of his family to serve Canada and the British Empire in wartime, nor was he the only one to do so during the Second World War. After coming to Canada from Henley-on-Thames, England, in 1890 at age 17, his father William—my grandfather—served with the Canadian contingent that aided the British Army during the Boer War. After returning from South Africa to his homestead near Summerberry, Saskatchewan, William married Agnes McCowan, whose family had left Dumfries, Scotland, for Liverpool, England, moved to Australia, resettled in New Zealand, and finally homesteaded in the Summerberry district after arriving in Canada.[1] The couple had four children: Jennie Ellen, born 1911; William Jeffries, born 1913; James, born 1917; and George McCowan, born 1922. During the Second World War, Jennie, more commonly known as Jeanne,

---

1   Information relating to the King and McCowan family histories can be found in *Bridging the Past: Wolseley and District, 1880-1980* and Galbraith, Iva W. and Iris Smith, eds. *Centennial Tribute: The Story of Broadview and Area.*

married Friend Bruce Sitter of Wilkie, and William Jeffries (Bill) remained at home to run the farm with his parents. George and James both enlisted in the RCAF at Regina, and James served as a Leading Aircraftman in Coastal Command in the Maritimes and Newfoundland until the end of the war. About six months after George and James enlisted, their cousin James McCowan—the son of Agnes' older brother James—was posthumously awarded his pilot's wings after being killed on a training flight while attending No. 11 Elementary Flying Training School at Yorkton in May of 1942.[2] Of the seven servicemen from the Summerberry district killed during the Second World War, then, two were from the King and McCowan families.[3]

Born on the family farm two miles northeast of Summerberry on 19 April 1922, George McCowan King had a typical rural Canadian upbringing. Like most farm children of his generation, he had to perform a daily regimen of chores but still found time to socialise in the district. He hunted, went with friends to dances in town, and played a variety of sports, including hockey, curling, and his favourite, baseball. George was a bit undisciplined in his studies at Summerberry School, on at least one occasion being forced to conceal his grades from his parents by shoving his report card down a

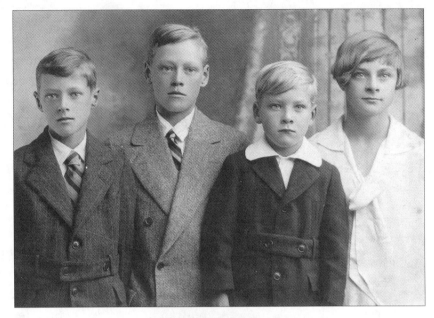

Above, the King children, circa 1928: from left to right, James, Bill, George, and Jeannie.

Left, Sergeant Pilot James Gordon McCowan, circa 1942.

---

2 In 1994, the Government of Manitoba named McCowan Lake in northern Manitoba after James Gordon McCowan.

3 Seven World War II servicemen are memorialised on the cenotaph at Summerberry: George King, James McCowan, Ken Bourne, James Main, John Slabiak, Stan Sotkowy, and William Hollingshead. All were killed in wartime except William Hollingshead, who died of pneumonia in Nova Scotia in 1947 after returning from overseas.

Photos clockwise from top left: George King on the farm near Summerberry, circa 1927; George and his brother Jim on the farm, circa 1927; the King children with their uncle, circa 1925: left to right, Les McCowan, Jim, Jeannie, Bill (wearing hat), and George; the King family on the farm, circa 1935: left to right, Annie Taylor, Bill, Agnes, Jim, William, and George.

gopher hole on the way home from school. Nonetheless, he graduated from grade twelve in 1939, and worked on the family farm until he and his brother James enlisted in the RCAF at No. 5 Recruiting Centre, Regina, on 29 November 1941.

Like many other recruits, George and James carefully considered their options as servicemen, and came up with several reasons to enlist in the RCAF rather than in one of the other branches of the Canadian Armed Forces. For one thing, given their father's experience in the Boer War, they probably felt that the Air Force provided a more detached and thus potentially less grisly and disturbing means of engaging with the enemy than did either the Canadian Army or Navy. As well, although they could potentially move around Canada and England a fair bit during both training and operations, as airmen they would always be based on land at either an RCAF or an RAF station. Their accommodations might be somewhat spartan, but members of the Air Force could reasonably expect to eat and sleep more regularly—if not a bit better—than their counterparts who served either at sea or in the field. By late 1941, when George and James joined up, the Air Force "seemed to be the service making the biggest contribution to beating the enemy,"[4] and Allan D. English states that at a time when air travel was a far less common phenomenon than it is today, Air Force service had an excitement and a glamour about it that tempted many young Canadians.[5] It most certainly held a special allure for two brothers from rural Saskatchewan who had spent their entire lives to that point working on the land.

His initial posting as an Aircraftman 2 at No. 2 Manning Depot at Brandon, Manitoba, on 16 December 1941 quickly disabused George of any notions he had had of the glamorous RCAF life. The various manning depots across the country served almost as "boot camps," their primary function being to teach recruits the rudiments of military discipline—waking up early in the morning, polishing their boots and caring for their uniforms, learning how to march, undergoing physical training, and even serving on

---

4   Dunmore, *Wings*, 173.

5   English, *Cream*, 13.

guard duty—all for 40 dollars per month.[6] After roughly a month and a half at Brandon Manning Depot where he made the transition from civilian recruit to fledgling airman, George was posted to No. 7 Bombing and Gunnery School (B.G.S.) at Paulson, Manitoba, on 1 February 1942. On 14 February, he returned to Brandon, this time to attend No. 12 Service Flying Training School (S.F.T.S). At the end of March, he was transferred back to Saskatchewan, and as a student in No. 4 Training Command, he began No. 2 Initial Training School (I.T.S.) at Regina.

During their time at I.T.S., recruits got their first real taste of aviation—albeit on the ground—in the form of a series of courses on flying, navigation, gunnery, meteorology, Morse code, and wireless operation. Based on an interview and their marks in these courses, airmen were then selected for their specific jobs in aircrews. Typically, the top 20 percent of students in the class became navigators, largely because navigators were required to perform many complex calculations in determining the location and course of their aircraft. The next 20 percent of students became bomb aimers, with the next two groups of students becoming pilots and air gunners, respectively.[7] Having done well on his exams, George was promoted to Leading Aircraftman and chosen as a potential navigator. When George graduated to No. 3 Air Observer School (A.O.S.) at Regina in July of 1942, his Commanding Officer at I.T.S. had this to say about him:

> *A quiet, capable young airman who had no difficulty on the course. While he did not make outstanding marks he should have no difficulty in qualifying for a Navigator as he appears to apply himself constantly. He is rather youthful, but shows fair leadership qualities.*

George began A.O.S. Air Navigator Course No. 54 at Regina on 5 July 1942 and flew in an aircraft for the first time on 18 July. His log book indicates that while flying in twin-engined Avro Anson bombers, for the next three months he studied all facets of air

---

6   McCaffery, *Battlefields*, 65–6.
7   Zinkhan, "Aircrew," B10.

navigation: taking astronomical readings, calculating airspeed and drift, using a compass, charting a course, and pinpointing landmarks on the ground. After No. 3 A.O.S. moved from Regina to Pearce, Alberta, in September of 1942, George continued his Air Navigator Course at Pearce. By the time he completed the course, he had logged 115 hours in the air, 43 of them at night, and he graduated from A.O.S. as an Air Navigator with the rank of Sergeant on 23 October 1942. After he underwent three altitude tests on 11 November 1942 and was authorised to fly at 35,000 feet and above, George travelled by train to No. 1 "Y" Depot at Halifax, Nova Scotia,[8] where he waited to be posted to a ship travelling overseas to England. At this point he began writing the letters home which comprise the first half of this book.

On 22 November, George embarked for England from Halifax, and after eight days at sea, his ship—fortunate enough not to be torpedoed by a German U-boat, as occasionally happened—docked at Plymouth, England, on 30 November. From there,

---

8   "Y" Depot was an Overseas Transit Depot, where servicemen were posted before embarking for overseas duty.

Graduation from A.O.S., Pearce, Alberta, October 1942. Above, George is in middle row, second from right. Below, George is fifth from the left. An Avro Anson training aircraft is in the background.

George was sent to a Canadian holding depot at the southern resort town of Bournemouth, where he waited a month for his initial posting in England. Having received leave for Christmas, he spent the holiday in Henley-on-Thames with his Uncle George as well as his widowed Aunt Daisey and her three grown children—his cousins—Phil, Tom, and Kathleen. He also visited his aunts Sallie and Lottie King in London as well as his friend Ken Bourne before returning to Bournemouth. In early January 1943, he was posted to No. 9 Elementary Flying Training School (E.F.T.S.) at Ansty, Warwickshire, where he flew in de Havilland Tiger Moth training aircraft and continued his training in map reading. After completing his course in the middle of February, he returned to the holding depot at Bournemouth to await a further posting.

In late March, he went on leave and again visited his aunts in London, and then in early April proceeded to No. 3 Advanced Flying Unit (A.F.U.) at Bobbington, Staffordshire. There, he passed his night vision test on 2 April, and on 23 April he was promoted to the rank of Flight Sergeant. On 14 April he began No. 72 Air Observers Advanced Navigation Course. Once again flying in Ansons, he trained mainly in pinpointing landmarks on the ground, and on 11 May, he was certified as having completed the course. He was immediately posted to No. 30 Operational Training Unit (O.T.U.) at Hixon, Staffordshire, to complete his training as a navigator. In late May, he wrote a series of exams and then began a variety of navigational exercises in twin-engined Vickers Wellington "Wimpy" bombers. At this time, he joined up with four of his crewmates: Pilot Norman Spencer of Vancouver, Air Gunner William Baker of Toronto, Bomb Aimer Douglas Wylie of Toronto, and Wireless Operator Harold Hicks of Cardiff, Wales. When he completed his time at O.T.U. on 18 July, George was recommended for a commission, meaning that he would soon advance to the rank of Flying Officer.

George again spent his leave visiting his relatives at Henley and in London before being posted to No. 1652 Conversion Unit (C.U.) at Waterbeach, Cambridgeshire, on 23 July. Training in this C.U., he took his first flights in four-engined Stirling Mk. III heavy bombers in order to familiarise himself with the larger aircraft before joining an operational squadron. At that time, he met the final two members of his crew, Mid-

Upper Gunner Raymond Eberle of Toronto, and Flight Engineer William Morement of Preston, England. By late August of 1943, having completed his training and logged a total of 261 hours in the air, 106 of them at night, George was qualified to fly operations. With the rest of his aircrew, he was attached to an RAF squadron of 3 Group—218 (Gold Coast) Squadron, based at Downham Market, Norfolk. Given the fact that George would be killed on operations within a month, it is rather fitting that 218 Squadron's badge was an hour-glass with "the golden sand having almost run through."[9] At any rate, since 3 Group was at that time comprised largely of Stirlings,[10] and since George's C.U. training had been in these aircraft, if all went well he would fly in Stirlings for the duration of his tour of duty, which might entail anywhere from 30 to 40 operations over France and Germany.

By 1943, however, Stirling heavy bombers, their design having been completed in 1938 to RAF Specification B.12/36, were "already revealing themselves as disappointments" in operations over Germany.[11] Air Marshal Sir Arthur Harris himself would later call them "the least efficient of the four-engined bombers,"[12] largely because their compartmentalised bomb bays did not allow them to carry bombs weighing more than 2000 pounds.[13] Harris further characterised Stirlings—the first RAF four-engined heavy bombers—as being "hopelessly out of date for any operation against a well-defended target,"[14] and in fact, they were outperformed by the recently

Stirling bomber, courtesy of the Canadian Forces / PL4960

---

9 Moyes, *Squadrons*, 212.

10 Middlebrook, *War Diaries*, 336.

11 Webster, *Strategic*, 92.

12 Harris, *Bomber*, 125.

13 Gunston, *Directory*, 464–5.

14 Harris, *Bomber*, 228.

developed Avro 683 Lancaster in almost every capacity, including "range, bombload, ease of handling, freedom from accident, and…casualty rate."[15] The Stirling's high casualty rate was due in part to a crucial shortcoming that it possessed but which was not as apparent in the Lancaster or the Halifax: a disproportionately short wingspan. Although capable of withstanding a considerable amount of punishment from enemy defences and still returning home despite having had one or more engines destroyed, Stirlings were more susceptible to enemy fire than Lancasters and Halifaxes for the simple fact that their inadequate wing area limited their operational ceiling. Although it was larger than the Lancaster since it was 87 feet long and had a cockpit height of over 22 feet, the Stirling had a wingspan which was relatively short for its size—99 feet long to allow it to fit inside standard RAF hangars—and as a result, the aircraft "had a poor ceiling and sluggish manoeuvrability except at low level."[16] Loaded with fuel and bombs, Stirlings typically operated at between 10,000 and 18,000 feet, far below the 24,500-foot service ceiling of Lancasters, and "would therefore attract all the flak, while the Lancasters would go comparatively free."[17] In fact, Spencer Dunmore reports that because the low-flying Stirling and Handley Page Halifax bombers attracted the majority of anti-aircraft fire, "many former Lancaster crewmen recall feeling intensely sorry for the Stirling and Halifax crews—yet secretly relieved when they would be coming along on a given night."[18] Quite simply, Stirlings were "much easier to shoot down" than other of the Allied bombers,[19] and the raid on Berlin on the night of 23–24 August 1943 demonstrated this when 12.9 percent of the operating Stirlings did not return to base,

---

15 Webster, *Strategic*, 92.

16 Gunston, *Directory*, 462; Ellis, *Encyclopedia*, 463. Although Lancasters and Halifaxes were also designed to RAF specification B.12/36, by the time they were delivered into service, the RAF had eliminated these peacetime limitations on wingspan.

17 Harris, *Bomber*, 135.

18 Dunmore, *Whirlwind*, 180.

19 McCaffery, *Battlefields*, 53.

compared with 5.4 percent of the Lancasters.[20] By the autumn of 1943, "the pattern of casualties told what was now becoming an increasingly familiar tale. While the Lancasters bore the brunt of the attack, the Halifaxes, and even more so the Stirlings, bore the brunt of the casualties."[21] The aircraft was by no means a "death-trap," but flying in a Stirling added an increased element of danger to the already dangerous practice of flying operations, and realising this, Bomber Command withdrew the Stirling from major operations over Germany in November of 1943.[22]

In August of 1943, however, when George began flying operations with 218 Squadron, the Stirling was still playing a substantial role in the air campaign against Germany. On the night of 23–24 August, for example, when Pilot Norman Spencer made his first operational flight in a Stirling as an observing pilot on the mission to Berlin, 124 of the 727 aircraft involved, and 16 of the 56 lost, were Stirlings.[23] George's log book records that after Spencer made his initial familiarising sortie to Berlin, the rest of the crew flew their first operation in a Stirling the next night—a relatively low-risk minelaying trip to the Frisian Islands off the Dutch coast that was meant to ease them into operations. Similarly, on the night of 25–26 August, the crew joined other aircraft "gardening" or laying mines in the Bay of Biscay, and themselves laid mines in the Gironde estuary heading upriver to Bordeaux, France. Although George and his crewmates would experience no great difficulties on these minelaying operations, and although no aircraft would be lost, things would change drastically the very next night when they were scheduled to join a raid on Nuremberg.[24] Having taken off from Downham Market, the crew's Stirling lost power in the port inner engine, and after circling back, the crew was forced to jettison fuel and bombs and make a dangerous

---

20 Webster, *Strategic*, 190.

21 Ibid., 163.

22 Ibid., 92.

23 Middlebrook, *War Diaries*, 425.

24 Allied aircrews could reasonably expect relatively few casualties when operating over Occupied Europe because Germany concentrated its air defences so as to protect Reich targets.

landing—3,000 pounds overweight and on three engines—back at base. Other crews were not so lucky; of the 104 Stirlings on the raid, 11 did not return.[25]

Their aircraft repaired, George's crew flew their next operation into Germany—this time to Mönchengladbach and the neighbouring town of Rheydt—the night of 30–31 August. For the crew in particular and for Bomber Command in general, this raid was more successful than the previous one: the bombing was especially accurate, and only 6 of 107 Stirlings were lost.[26] The eight-hour operation to Berlin the next night, however, would be another matter. Of the 622 combined aircraft taking part, 47 were lost, and of the 106 Stirlings that participated, 17—a staggering 16 percent—did not return, largely due to the "ferocity of German defences."[27] George and his crew's plane had a hole shot in one of its fuel tanks, but otherwise it returned unscathed. On 2 September, the crew received their own aircraft—denoted EF 139—which barring anything unforeseen was intended to last them for the duration of their time on operations. On their very next operation, a seven-hour return flight to Mannheim, Germany, on the night of 5–6 September, their new plane suffered minor damage on the way back to Downham Market, losing the cover to the pilot's escape hatch as well as the astro dome through which George as navigator was to take celestial sightings. Flying for over three hours in freezing temperatures, the crew nonetheless returned safely to base, but again, Stirling casualties were quite high; this time, 8 of 111 Stirlings taking part in the operation did not return to England.[28]

Not scheduled to fly any more operations for the next week, George obtained his leave on 7 September and travelled to Edinburgh with Bill Baker. The two then attended the wedding of Doug Wylie's brother in London before visiting George's relatives in Henley and returning to Downham Market to resume operations. The night of 15–16

---

25 Middlebrook, *War Diaries*, 426.

26 Ibid., 427.

27 Ibid., 427–8.

28 Ibid., 429.

September, George and his crewmates were part of a combined force of 369 aircraft that bombed the Dunlop rubber factory at Montluçon, France, and this time, the contingent of Stirlings fared quite well, with only 1 of 120 failing to return to base.[29] The next night when the crew flew with 339 other aircraft on an eight-hour return trip to Modane, France, the Stirling casualty rate was even less—1 lost out of 127.[30] On the night of 22–23 September, George's crew was part of a 711 aircraft force that operated over Hannover, Germany, but because of high winds, most of the aircraft missed their targets, and "it is unlikely that serious damage was caused."[31] Serious damage was caused, however, to the fabric of my family, for of the five Stirlings that did not return, one of them was George's.

After they learned on 25 September 1943 that George was missing on air operations, my family remained in one form of limbo or another for the next ten years. Initially, they held out hope that he had survived the crash and been taken prisoner of war, but on 14 November, they received word that he had lost his life on the night of 22 September. Almost a year later, on 12 November 1944, my grandparents received a carton containing George's personal effects, but this gave them little solace since they still did not know the particulars of his death. Over the next year and a half, they endured the painful process of settling George's affairs: after numerous correspondences back and forth with the Estates Branch in Ottawa, they received the balance of George's service estate in 1945 and his War Service Gratuity in 1946.

But due to both the number of Canadian servicemen killed overseas and the circumstances in Europe after the war, the most important question for my family—the location of George's grave—was to remain unresolved for several more years. In June of 1944, my grandfather wrote to the Department of National Defence for Air in Ottawa

---

29 Ibid., 430–1.

30 Ibid., 431.

31 Ibid., 432.

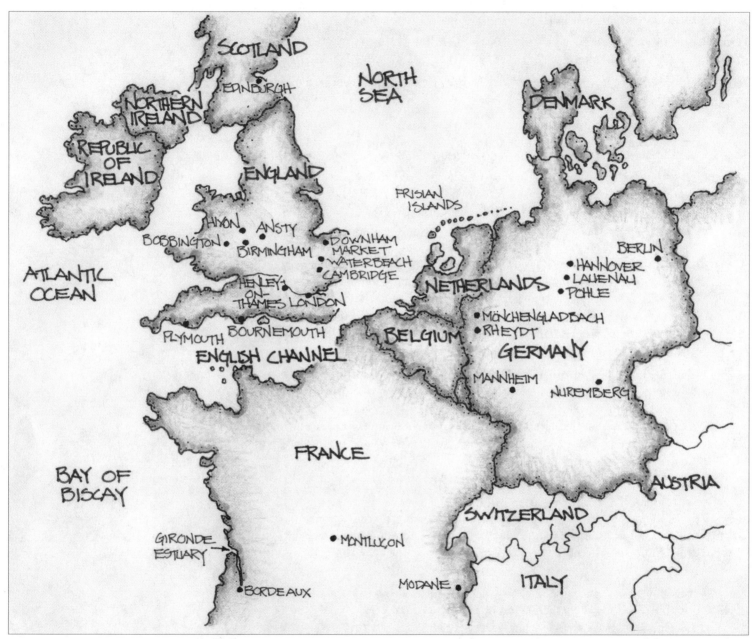

This map shows the locations relevant to George King's life and military service in 1943 / hand-drawn map by Neil Erickson.

seeking information about where George had been buried. In November of 1945, this request was forwarded to the RAF Missing Research and Enquiry Service,[32] and on 5 September 1946, Flight Lieutenant C.W. Lord, Investigation Officer for No. 24 Section, No. 4 Missing Research and Enquiry Unit,[33] sent the following report to the Air Ministry in London:

***

As instructed on Sept. 5, 1946, I proceeded to Pohle to investigate Casualty Enquiry No. G.229.

Aircraft:

I first interviewed Herr Braumes, former Burgermeister of Lauenau and he stated that a four-engined English bomber had been shot down [at] approximately 2330 hrs. on the night of Sept. 22nd, 1943, at Pohle. Upon arrival in Pohle I contacted Herr Noltemeier who was Burgermeister at the time of the crash. Herr Noltemeier stated that he was not at home at the time of the incident but that he knew where the a/c had been shot down. Herr Noltemeier (who was Burgermeister) also stated that he being Burgermeister at the time of the crash and not being home, his daughter, Frl. Noltemeier, was ordered by the Landrat at Springe to remove the identity discs and personal effects from the bodies.

Along with Frl. Noltemeier (who had arrived at the crashed aircraft at approx. 2340 hrs.), I proceeded to the scene of the crash. Frl. Noltemeier states having seen the aircraft shot down by a fighter while flying at a very low altitude. The bomber exploded in mid-air and broke in two parts. Both parts of the aircraft fell in a wheat-field ¾ of a mile south of Pohle and approx. 100 ft. on the west side of the main road leading to Meinsen from Pohle. The a/c did not burn and was salvaged and taken away by the Luftwaffe to Wunstorf.

Aircrew:

Frl. Noltemeier said that she had arrived at the scene 10 min. after the aircraft crashed. Other local residents gathered and two bodies were found that night lying close to the wreckage. Frl. Noltemeier again visited the scene of the crash at

---

32 The "Missing Research and Enquiry Service," or M.R.E.S., was the organisation charged with locating the graves of servicemen killed in action.

33 A Missing Research and Enquiry Unit, or M.R.E.U., was an individual team that conducted investigations into the location of the graves of deceased servicemen in Europe.

approx. 0800 hrs. on the morning of September 23rd. By this time local residents had found three more dead airmen within a distance of about 400 feet from the aircraft. At approx. 0900 hrs. Frl. Noltemeier began removing from the dead flyers identity discs and personal effects, having been ordered to do so by the Landrat at Springe.

Frl. Noltemeier stated that she remembered the name of one of the flyers very well. She said his name was HICKS and that she removed from him his identity discs, a snapshot of himself, and a newspaper clipping concerning himself. These along with valuables taken from the four other airmen were given to the Luftwaffe officer who arrived at the scene at approx. 1000 hrs.

I then interviewed Herr Klausing whom I had been told had made coffins for the dead airmen. Herr Klausing said he had made five coffins and that they were taken to the scene of the crash during the afternoon of Sept. 24th, 1943. He stated that he had helped place the bodies in the coffins, each airman in a separate one. He stated that none of the airmen were burned and that they were only slightly disfigured. Obtaining Herr Noltemeier's team of horses, he along with local residents took the five bodies to Lauenau for burial. He said that he remembered that there was one officer in the crew and that he had been buried in the centre position in the grave and that they had placed two coffins on each side of the officer's. No pastor was at the grave side and no service was held. A cross bearing no names nor dates was erected by local residents.

Exhumation:
In accordance with the new M.R.E.S. policy I did not carry out the exhumation as it is definite that the crew in question, all five airmen, are buried in the Lauenau Protestant Cemetery.

Conclusion:
There is no doubt in my mind that the airman whom Frl. Noltemeier said had been identified as HICKS was 1316957 Sgt. H.J. HICKS, A/B,[34] of the crew concerned. Herr Klausing also stated that only one of the five bodies had been identified as that of an officer. This body must therefore have been J.27315 P/O EBERLE, A/G, the only officer in the crew. This is sufficient evidence to prove

---

34 Harold Hicks was actually a Wireless Operator rather than an Air Bomber.

that the aircraft which crashed ¾ mi. south of Pohle at 2330 hrs. on the night of Sept. 22nd, 1943, was Stirling Mk. III EF 139.

Under the new scheme regarding exhumations, the bodies will possibly remain for some time where they are at present buried. When a G.C.U.[35] exhumes the bodies to concentrate them in a Military Cemetery, individual identity will most likely be established. I have arranged that the Burgermeister of Lauenau erects a cross bearing the names, numbers, and date of death of the members of the crew concerned.

***

The M.R.E.U. recorded the location of the grave, and a temporary cross was erected. On 26 November 1946, a different Investigation Officer, Flying Officer Seilern, went with a Graves Commission Unit to conduct a further investigation and perform the exhumation necessary to relocate the servicemen's remains to a military cemetery. Seilern's report differs from Lord's in some respects, but sheds further light on the fate of the aircrew:

***

RESULT OF INVESTIGATION AND FINDINGS:

Whilst carrying [out] investigations in Kreis Spring, I proceeded to the village of Lauenau where it was reported that five airmen, recovered from the crash of a four-engined bomber on the night of the 22nd September 1943, were buried in the local cemetery.

Aircraft:

According to Herr Nettelmann—an architect resident in Lauenau—an attack on Hannover was in progress during the night of 21/22 September 1943, and the aircraft in question, a four-engined bomber, approached Lauenau on the way back from the target at approximately 00.25 hours on 22.9.43.[36] It was

---

35 G.C.U. stands for Graves Commission Unit, a team responsible for organising the burial of deceased servicemen in military cemeteries.

36 Herr Nettelmann's account is incorrect with respect to the date and time that the George's plane crashed, but this is not surprising considering that he was interviewed more than three years after the fact.

intercepted by night fighters and burst into flames as the result of the attack. It then circled the village, losing height, and finally crashed in Germarkung Pohle which is just west of the village. It carried no bombs but there was a considerable amount of ammunition on board which was detonated as the result of the flames from the wreckage. Pieces of the machine were scattered over a wide area and the nose and the tail were [the] only parts which had not been completely destroyed by fire.

Aircrew:

Two bodies were recovered from the nose of the aircraft. Herr Nettelmann seemed to remember that one of them was later identified as HICKS. Another body was found about 300 metres from the aircraft, another 50–80 metres from the wreckage, and the fifth, badly burned and mutilated, close to the burnt out

The aircrew at O.T.U., summer 1943. Standing, left to right, Doug Wylie, Norm Spencer and George. Kneeling, left to right, Harold Hicks and Bill Baker.

aircraft. Two members of the crew were reported to have baled out—one of them possibly the rear gunner whose turret was found to be empty. It was thought that one of the survivors was suffering from a fractured collar bone. Both men were apprehended by the Wehrmacht who also undertook identification of the dead men and removed their personal belongings to the airfield at Hameln.

The burial of the five men took place about two days after the crash occurred. Each body was interred in a single coffin and placed in a communal grave on the eastern side of the village cemetery (no grave numbers are available). Only a few villagers were present at the burial and no military honour or church rituals were accorded since there were no Wehrmacht personnel in the area at the time and no pastor in Lauenau.

The grave appeared to be in good condition and had been registered by No. 24 Section, 4 M.R.E.U. who had supplied the following list of names which had [been] inscribed on the cross:

J.27315 P/O EBERLE R.E.

R.122306 SGT. SPENCER N.V.

R.142247 SGT. KING G.M.

R.129010 SGT. WYLIE D.M.

1316957 SGT. HICKS H.J.

Killed in Action 22.9.43

***

My grandparents would never learn these specific details about George's death and initial burial at Lauenau. In a letter of 28 January 1947, the RCAF provided them with basic details of the airplane crash, informed them that George had been buried in a communal grave at Lauenau, and said that he would eventually be reinterred in a military cemetery.[37] Six months later, in July of 1947, my family learned that George had been reinterred with two of his crewmates in a communal grave at Hannover-Limmer Military Cemetery. Since the crewmen had not yet been individually identified, my grandparents still did not know the exact location of George's grave, nor did they ever learn that, as the exhumation report states, George had been reburied with the CANADA flash on his original uniform "still intact."

My family eventually did learn more about the location of George's remains. In May of 1949, the Chief of the Air Staff for the RCAF sent them two photographs of the temporary cross that had been erected at George's graveside, and in 1951—a year after my grandfather's death—my family learned that George's final resting-place had been registered as Grave 2, Row H, Plot 2, of the British Military Cemetery at Hannover-Limmer. In 1953—ten years after George's death—they learned that the Imperial War Graves Commission had erected a permanent memorial on George's grave. My grandmother never fully came to terms with George's death, but she received some degree of closure in 1961; that year, as part of Saskatchewan's Geo-memorial Project, the Provincial Government recognised George's sacrifice by naming a creek in northern Saskatchewan after him. My grandmother took comfort in the fact that although her youngest son was buried overseas, he would forever remain a part of the province and country for which he so selflessly gave his life.

"Your Loving Son": Letters of an RCAF Navigator, although comprised of many voices, forms a coherent narrative that leads up to, documents, and explores the repercussions of George's death on the night of 22 September 1943. Focusing on the period from late 1942 to the end of the war, but extending even into the 1990s, the voices that combine

---

37 See Letter 122.

to tell the story of George McCowan King's life and death as an RCAF airman are many: his letters; my father's letters; my grandparents' correspondence with the families of other servicemen and with sympathetic friends; diary and logbook entries; even official government missives concerning the circumstances of my uncle's death and the naming of "King Creek." Because of this variety of sources, *"Your Loving Son"* gives a number of perspectives on the Second World War, but its real value lies in the fact that it reveals some of the powerful emotions felt by many servicemen: regret at leaving home and family, longing for the simple pleasures of home, excitement at leaving small towns in Canada for adventure in Europe, trepidation at facing possible death there, shock at having lost friends in war, and pride at having served Canada in a time of great need. Since all of the letters that George received do not survive, and since he was himself constrained by military censors regarding what he could include in his own letters, there are inevitable gaps in the narrative, but these gaps do not detract from the overall picture. Rather, they enhance it by illustrating that there are innumerable aspects of wartime life experienced by servicemen and their families—loneliness, fear, shock, and sorrow—which those of later generations can barely begin to comprehend at a remove of almost sixty years. Beginning as my uncle left Canada for England, chronicling his training and commencement of operations against Germany, and continuing through to his death and its aftermath, this book opens a small window into what the Second World War meant to Canadians who experienced it firsthand.

The first half of this book is comprised largely of letters which George wrote to his parents at home on the farm and to his brother serving in the Maritimes and Newfoundland while he himself underwent training and eventually began participating in night operations against Germany. Although his letters to each audience are quite different from each other, they all combine to illustrate some of the emotions felt by those who served overseas during the war. The letters to his family at home convey many of the feelings which a young serviceman would express to his parents—concern for their welfare, excitement at having visited their hometown in England, happiness at having met relatives in the old country, eagerness to return home to work on the farm, and a reluctance to discuss his air operations. The letters to his brother James, my father, tell rather a different story; in addition to expressing the excitement of a twenty-year-old at having travelled to England for the first time, they also voice some of the concerns of many young servicemen stationed in a new country—the quality of the food, the availability of cigarettes and liquor, the possibility of meeting young women, and the frustration at having to cope with military censorship. And as is characteristic of many airmen's letters of the period, they show a firm faith in his crewmates and aircraft, as well as a bravado which may have belied his true feelings about operating against the enemy.

The remainder of the book documents the aftermath of George's death. Letters from sympathetic relatives, friends, and the families of George's fellow airmen give some hint of the grief which his immediate family—and the families of thousands of other Canadian servicemen—felt first upon hearing that their son had been reported missing, and then upon learning that he had been killed. A story in the local newspaper demonstrates how countless neighbourhoods and small communities were affected by the death of some of their most popular youths. The letters from RCAF and government officials tell a slightly different story. With their terseness and reluctance (or inability) to provide details regarding George's death, these letters show a characteristic detachment, but one which must have been necessary given the sheer number of such letters that had to be sent to grieving families.[38] These official letters give an idea of the frustration felt by their recipients—the frustration of not knowing exactly what had happened to their sons, and of having to wait years to learn precisely where they had been buried. In the midst of these necessarily terse letters, however, are some letters that are remarkable for their compassion, most notably those written by the RCAF chaplain who conducted the funeral services for both George and his cousin James McCowan. Excerpts from the diary of one of George's fellow airmen provide a glimpse into George's final days, and give some idea of the conditions under which airmen flew operations. Closing the main body

---

38 Casualty information had to be passed from German authorities to the International Red Cross and then to the RAF, so in many cases the Air Ministry had little to report to the families of missing servicemen.

of the book, George's logbook provides additional details of his operations against Germany, and adds an element of cold finality to his life in the RCAF. To end the book, the letters which comprise the epilogue detail the number of memorials which exist to George McCowan King, the sort of memorials that many servicemen's families do not realise exist for their own loved ones in addition to their local cenotaph.

As the editor of these letters, I cannot be called the author of this book by any stretch of the imagination. The story which they tell was written a long time before I was even born, and my role simply was to collect, organise, and transcribe the documents so that they can tell it on their own with as little editorial intervention as possible. The letters do this remarkably well. They needed only occasional editing for grammatical purposes, and some silent editing of punctuation, as is often required when dealing with handwritten work composed in such difficult circumstances. The letters of servicemen and their families provide invaluable insight into the social history of Canada during the wars of the past century, largely because they take into account the human cost of war that more academic histories often overlook. And at a time when transitory and often impersonal telephone and e-mail exchanges are undermining the lasting and personal practice of letter writing, these letters represent an increasingly rare but especially expressive part of our historical record.

The story which this book tells is not an original one at all. In fact, it is all too common, which is part of its tragic nature. There is hardly a person of my father's generation who did not lose—or at least know someone who lost—a family member in either of the two great wars of the past century. And most members of my generation can recall that there was some branch of their family tree which was sadly cut short during one of the wars. This book tells a story which veterans and their immediate families refuse to forget, and if the turnout I witness at Remembrance Day ceremonies every year is any indication, it tells a story of heroism and sacrifice which younger Canadians both wish and need to hear.

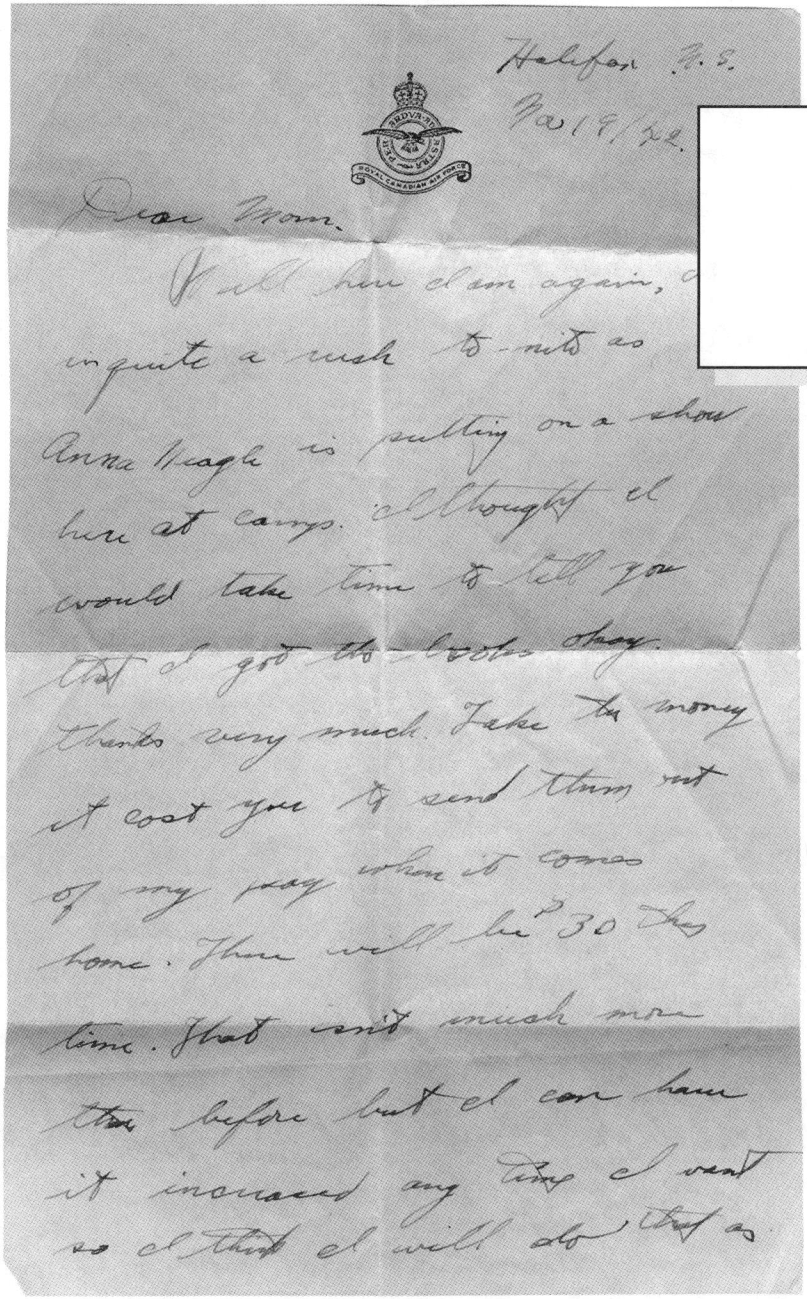

Halifax N.S.
Nov 19/42.

Dear Mom.
Well here I am again, a
in quite a rush to-nite as
Anna Neagle is putting on a show
here at camp. I thought I
would take time to tell you
that I got the books okay.
thanks very much. Take the money
it cost you to send them out
of my pay when it comes
home. There will be $30 this
time. That isn't much more
than before but I can have
it increased any time I want
so I think I will do that as

Prologue:

"From Canada"

LETTER 1.

R142247
SGT. KING G.M.
Halifax, N.S.
November 19th, 1942

Dear Mom,

Well here I am again. I'm in quite a rush tonite as Anna Neagle* is putting on a show here at camp. I thought I would take time to tell you that I got the books okay. Thanks very much. Take the money it cost you to send them out of my pay when it comes home. There will be $30 this time. That isn't much more than before but I can have it increased any time I want so I think I will do that as soon as I see how much I need in a month over there.

I'm sending my overseas address this time as you can never tell when I will get moved and it would take a long time for me to get a letter if you had to wait till I got a letter back to you.

Things are much the same here. I met young Les† pretty near as soon as he got here. It was sure nice to see him. We were out together last nite. I hope you are all well at home and the weather is nice. It is rather damp and foggy here.

Can. R142247
Sgt. King G.M.
R.C.A.F.
Overseas

Your loving son,
George.

* Anna Neagle (1904-1986) was one of the most famous English box office stars of the 1940s. Her director and future husband, Herbert Wilcox, had served in the Royal Flying Corps under Billy Bishop during World War I. In 1942, Bishop—now an Air Marshal—convinced Wilcox and Neagle to tour Canada in a production called "Celebrity Parade." By the time Neagle returned to England in late 1942, through the tour she had helped to raise $245 000 for the war effort (Neagle, *Autobiography*, 139–42). George is probably referring to a performance of "Celebrity Parade" that Neagle gave immediately before she left Canada from Halifax.

† "Young Les" was Agnes King's nephew, the son of her brother Malcolm (Mac) McCowan. Les served overseas in the Air Force during the war.

George and his cousins, circa 1928. Left to right, James McCowan, "Young Les" McCowan, Joe Mills, and George.

to get them. The novelty wears off
fairly fast but it is always some
a person is proud of anyway

I guess I told you before that I
am back up in the Midlands and
navigating again. I rather enjoy it
it is rather nice to get flying
again and to get back to work.
and we really do work and when
we fly we really do that too. Two
times in a day. They are the same
kind of aircraft as I flew in at
Pearce and Regina. I still have
quite a bit of training to do before
I'm ready for anything. I must
say they really make sure a
person knows their stuff before
they get doing anything.

I got a letter from Aunt Dais
to-day she wants to know

Chapter 1:
"Quite a Bit of Training to Do"

LETTER 2.

R142247
SGT. KING G.M.
R.C.A.F. OVERSEAS
December 5th, 1942

Dear Jim,*

Well, old cock, here I am again, not quite so prompt as usual, but still slinging the same old stuff.

I've been here since the 1st and have been all eyes ever since. It's sure a swell country—everything green as hell right in December. The people are real friendly, and you can buy practically anything you want here at the same price you used to in Canada. Cigarettes are 2 cents each. You can get 10 a day and they are really God awful tasting things, but I got a great supply of Players in Canada and a lot of Camels and Chesterfields on the boat for 8 cents for 20, so I'm quite well-heeled for a while.

The supply of liquor is quite good. I've been here four nights and been drunk two, so that's not bad.

The food here is damn good. That stuff at Halifax was pig swill compared to this. This is real good and lots of it, and then you can get fish and chips or lots of other things for a lunch at nite.

There isn't a hell of a lot I can tell you, as it would be cut out anyway. Young Les came over on the same boat and I never saw him. He isn't at the same place as I am now, so I don't know when I'll be seeing him again.

I met Bob Scofield† last night, so we celebrated old times. He slings the same amount of shit as he ever did.

I'll have to write to Ken Bourne‡ and Soup and Lawrence§ and

Jim and George on the farm, circa 1941.

* George sent this letter, like the later ones he addressed to "Jim," to his brother James King, stationed in Atlantic Canada.

† Bob Scofield was a serviceman from the Summerberry district. Although Summerberry itself was never more than a village, and is in fact now a virtual ghost town, a large number of young men from the town and surrounding farms served in the military, as the letters demonstrate.

‡ Ken Bourne was an RCAF serviceman from the Summerberry district who was killed on operations on the night of 13 August 1943.

§ Lawrence McMain was a serviceman whose family farmed near the Kings.

* Ted Smith, Ted Box, and Stu Crawford were all servicemen from the Summerberry district.

† "That woman of mine" refers to Patricia (Patsy) Kerr, George's girlfriend at home, with whom he had a tempestuous relationship. She was the daughter of the United Church minister in Summerberry.

‡ "Poor Jim" refers to George's cousin, James McCowan, the son of Agnes' brother James and his wife May. James was killed on a training flight on 11 May 1942 while training as a pilot at No. 11 S.F.T.S. at Yorkton, Saskatchewan.

§ A "48" was what servicemen commonly called a two-day leave.

** Although because of censorship George was not able to say where he was stationed initially, when he first arrived in England, he was stationed on the southern coast at Bournemouth, a former holiday resort which was used as a holding depot for new Canadian arrivals overseas. He was stationed there for a little over a month.

†† "Buck" Fisher was an airman from Wadena. He was a friend of George's, and went missing on operations in 1944, although he made it back to England without being taken prisoner. Airmen such as this who avoided capture with the help of resistance sympathisers were known as "evaders."

‡‡ At this point in the letter, George changes from using YMCA paper to using issued RCAF paper.

find out where they are. Some of them may not be so far from me.

I guess you and old Ted Smith will have seen one another a few times by the time you get this letter. How about Ted Box and Stu?*

I guess that woman of mine† will be safe to have herself a shit of a good time now. Too bad you couldn't get home for Xmas just so you could send a report to me. I guess you'll kick the bung out of the barrel, as poor Jim‡ said. I think I'll finish this letter later as there is fuck all else I can think of right now.

Well, I laid off for a day, got pissed last night, and went to my first English dance. It was pretty good. Outside of a wild bloody beer session, what did you do for amusement on that last 48 you had?§

You can sure as hell have a lot of fun over here, and the climate is real nice. I guess this is one of the nicest spots in England.**

I think we will get our pay tomorrow or Tues. I have over 2 weeks' pay coming now.

There sure as hell isn't much to tell. I can't tell where I am, or what I'm doing, so that really cuts out plenty. Old Sgt. Goucher from Brandon Manning Depot is our Sgt. I guess you had him for a while, didn't you?

Young Fisher†† is going all to hell. He was drunk last night.

This paper suits me better than that "Y" shit,‡‡ but it was good of them to supply it when this wasn't handy.

I have had a couple of games of billiards and won both. They have damn good tables here.

I guess you will get 5 days at Xmas. I don't think we get any, but we can have a hell of a time here, and it's about the nicest place you can be in this country and we are all together here. I saw a little wine shop with gin, beer, whisky, wine, etc. in it today. We'll have to call on that before Xmas.

Today is Sunday, but the picture shows go on just the same, so we went out and saw one this afternoon. It was a pretty good show. You can smoke in these theatres, and they have such a good ventilation system you never see or smell the smoke, and everyone is smoking to beat hell.

This blackout is a bastard. I was running down the street to beat hell last night and ran into a bloody lamp post and fuckin' near broke my wrist. Of course, I was slightly under the weather when I did it, but I'm damn sure I wouldn't have ran[sic] into it in good light.*

I guess this is all I have to say for this time, but I'll be writing again soon.

> Your loving brother,
> George.

LETTER 3.

> George King†
> 50 Mount View
> Henley-on-Thames
> Oxon., England
> December 11th, 1942

Dear George,

I was very pleased and surprised to get a letter from you and to hear that you had arrived in England all safe and to hear that all was well at home. You must come and see me as soon as you can. I shall be glad to see you and hear all about how you are getting on and about all your family. Hoping to see you very soon, I remain

> Your loving Uncle,
> George

* In letter 13, George gives his parents a considerably toned down version of this event.

† George King, William King's brother, was George's uncle and namesake who lived at Henley-on-Thames, the city where William King grew up.

LETTER 4.

R142247
SGT. KING G.M.
R.C.A.F. OVERSEAS
December 15th, 1942

Dear Mom,

Here I am again trying airgraph this time. I can't send much, but I think it's fast. Please tell me if it is good. I am getting some Xmas leave and am going to see Uncle George and Aunt Sally.* I got a very prompt reply to my letter to Uncle George, and he is very anxious to have me come. I haven't heard from Aunt Sally yet. I have also received letters from Lawrence McMain and Ken Bourne. Lawrence and I are quite close, so we'll be seeing one another. I like England very much, and am having a good time. Money does not go far here, but I don't do bad. I guess it is quite cold at home by now. It is very nice here. I hope you are all well. Give my love to all.

Your loving son,
George.

LETTER 5.

R142247
SGT. KING G.M.
R.C.A.F. OVERSEAS
December 16th, 1942

Dear Mom, Dad and Bill,†

Here I am again, still at the same place. I still like England fine. The weather is nice here, but today it is very, very wet.

* Sallie King, William King's older sister, lived in Hampstead, a district of London. She stayed in Hampstead with her older sister Lottie for most of the war, but later went to Henley to stay with her sister-in-law, Daisey King.

† Bill King, 1913-1997, George's eldest brother, worked on the family farm during the war.

I have received a letter from Uncle George. He answered me as soon as I wrote, and seemed very anxious for me to go and see him. As I have 9 days leave at Xmas, I will be able to, alright. If Aunt Sally would write, I could go and see her too, but travelling is very hard in this country at Xmas—so many are going on leave. I am beginning to wonder if Aunt Sally is still in London or I would have heard from her by now.

I can have a good time over here, but money goes so awfully fast.

I think I will enclose Uncle George's letter just to show Dad he does write. It isn't big, but it was really prompt.

I am going to send you and the Sitter family* my Xmas greetings today by cable. It just costs 2 and 6 for that kind of a cable.†

I enjoy walking down by the ocean. Doug King‡ and I walked along it for about three miles the other day—it was really nice.

This nine days' leave is almost too much over here in England at Xmas time when there are travelling restrictions. I wish I could give about 5 days to Jim and then he could get home.

After I send this cable tonite, that will make 2 cables, 2 letters, and one airgraph, so you should be satisfied with my correspondence. I hope Holly§ got the photos to you okay. That will sort of serve as Xmas greetings for me, as the time of year rather tied my hands up for Xmas when I moved.

I have not received any mail from Canada yet, but have had 3 letters from over here—Uncle George, Lawrence, and Ken.

It is hard to realize Xmas is so close. It isn't advertised over here like they do in Canada.

I can get 2 choc[o]late bars a week over here. You can buy cigarettes and tobacco, but they are very expensive and not very nice tasting. I have some pipe tobacco and cigarettes left from my supply I brought from Canada.

* "The Sitter family" refers to George's sister Jeannie (1911-1989) and her husband, Friend Bruce Sitter. They operated a drugstore in Wilkie, Saskatchewan.

† "2 and 6" refers to two shillings sixpence.

‡ Douglas King was no relation to the Summerberry Kings. He was an airman whose family farmed near Pontrilas, Saskatchewan.

§ William Hollingshead was a serviceman whose family farmed in the Summerberry district. He was supposed to send George's pictures home, but did not do so immediately.

George on the farm, circa 1941.

How are you making out with the wood this winter? Is Bill getting any rabbits or anything hunting? How is Dad feeling these days? Are the two white heifers still milking? I hope I get an answer for all these questions.

The people here appear a bit funny to me. They are so hard to talk to, especially the girls at the dances—all they'll say is "yes" or "no." After a few attempts to talk, I mostly shut up, too.

I guess you are lucky if you have had breakfast yet. It will be about 7.10 your time, but I have had dinner and I guess I have to go on parade again, so I'll finish this up later.

Nothing new has happened, so I guess I may as well get this posted. I sent a cable home, and one to Jeannie today.

Love to all,
George.

LETTER 6.

C.P. Telegraphs
R142247
SGT. KING G.M.
R.C.A.F. OVERSEAS
December 22nd, 1942

Mrs. Wm. King, Summerbury[sic]:

Love and best wishes for Christmas and New Years to all at home. All well.

George King

LETTER 7.

R142247
SGT. KING G.M.
R.C.A.F. OVERSEAS
January 2nd, 1943

Dear Mother, Dad & Bill,

Here I am again, just back off leave. I was in Henley for 5 days and had a really grand time with Uncle George. He showed me all over the old haunts where my father commited[sic] all his evil as a boy, and I did get a few more reports of his escapades. I stayed at Aunt Daisie's* at night and had breakfast there and would then go and spend the day with Uncle George. We had a nice Xmas dinner at Auntie's— turkey and everything.

Tom† is looking very fat and healthy, but he has T.B. He is a fire watcher.‡ It's funny, but he remembered all about our place—even all the horses' names.

Uncle George looks very well. I believe he was a bit inclined to strut about town with his Canadian nephew. I met several of Dad's old friends—Charlie (Bummy) Bailey in particular, also Jack Banbury, Jim Gurdon, Edie Russell, Topper Bolton, Stump Buckett, [and] Mrs Hughs (Scannie Hughs' widow). We also went sightseeing and saw the Hop Gardens, Back. Fields, Marsh Lock and Weir, and the last day we went for a walk down the Fair Mile.§

I got eight letters from Canada when I got back off my leave—they had all been sent to Halifax. I hope you got my Xmas cable on time. Doug King just got an air mail letter from home written on the 21st of Dec., and they hadn't got his cable that he had got here, and he sent it the same day I did. That was the 2nd, I believe. I hope you got mine

* Daisey King, of Henley, was William King's sister-in-law. Her husband, William's brother, had died by 1942. I have not been able to determine his name.

† Tom was Daisey King's son, and thus George's cousin.

‡ The Fire Watcher Service had been formed in September 1940 to spot and report the fall of incendiaries and their ensuing fires.

§ Hop Gardens, the Back Fields, Marsh Lock and Weir, and the Fair Mile are all places in Henley which William King had told George about. Hop Gardens and the Fair Mile are streets in Henley, and the Marsh Lock and Weir is the lock at Henley on the river Thames. The Back Fields was an open space on the outskirts of the city which has since been developed, according to Philip Grahame, formerly of Henley.

*   Ralph Fleming was yet another serviceman from the Summerberry district.

†   "Young Feniak" refers to Fred Feniak, a serviceman from Grenfell, the town located eight miles due east of Summerberry.

‡   Bill Kenny, from Wolseley—the town located seven miles due west of Summerberry—was another serviceman friend of George's.

§   Frank and Minnie Hollingshead farmed near the Kings. Two of their sons—George and William Royal—served in World War II. William, an RCAF Leading Aircraftman, was stationed in Atlantic Canada for much of the war, and married a woman named Doris from Sydney, Nova Scotia. He died in Sydney in 1947 after developing pneumonia on the ship coming back from England.

**   George has just crossed out three attempts at spelling "brother's."

††   "G.C." refers to George's uncle, Gordon Campbell McCowan, who was Agnes' younger brother. Gordon's wife was Ellen, and his three daughters were Norma (born 1928), Jean (born 1929), and Barbara (born 1942). Gordon both farmed and operated the United Grain Growers' elevator at Summerberry.

‡‡   William and Agnes King's wedding anniversary was on 31 December.

faster than that. I had left Halifax the day before you wrote your letter to me there.

Ralph Fleming* heard I was over here, so he came to the city on a chance he would see me, and this is a fair-sized city, too, and he just walked into the picture show about 4 feet ahead of me. That's quite a thing, seeing there is[sic] about 7 different shows in town. It was nice to see Ralph—he is looking fine. Ken Bourne and I arranged a meeting and had a day together in London. Ken is really looking fine—it was sure good to see him. Lawrence McMain was going to come and see me, but his pass got mixed up, and he didn't get [it]. I met young Feniak† from Grenfell and Bill Kenny‡ from Wolseley, so I have seen quite a few of the boys.

I guess Mrs Hollingshead§ was referring to Bill's brother's (I can't spell it)** love affair, but it broke up just before I left. I saw the female and didn't tell Bill, but I'm far more ready to congratulate him on the breakup than ever starting it. I hope that they fixed Bill's Army call-up okay.

I hope it's not too cold over there, but your[sic] lucky it isn't this damp cold—it goes right through me. I have been forced to my warm woollies. I hope you had a good Xmas. I really had a dandy at Aunt Dais's. She is awfully good, but it amused me to hear her call me dear and kiss me good night and good morning.

I would like to get flying again. My feet have been on the ground so long now I'm going to take root one of these days.

Where was Xmas this year? It was at G.C.'s†† last if I remember correctly. I'm sorry I couldn't do anything about presents, cards, or anything, but I was thinking of you all. I also remembered your wedding anniversary,‡‡ but nothing could be done about that except a wire, and that would have been rather close to the Xmas one. I sent

Sitters a cable at Xmas, too.

I'm still with Fisher and all the other boys, so we still all go out together.

Those airgraph forms seem to be the only thing I can get hold of here, and I don't know just how fast they are.

I still have a few of my American cigarettes left, but they are getting fewer, and these English ones aren't very good. Some good Canadian fine cut and papers would come in handy.

I had a letter from Riley* and he doesn't like it over here now. So far, I still like it fine, but when the time comes to go back, I don't think I'll stay. I just ran out of Canadian writing paper. This is lovely stuff, isn't it? The food is okay, but what I couldn't do with two fried eggs. That's the only thing I miss.

How are Gordons† and Uncle Jims‡ and Mains?§ Remember me to them all. I have a heck of a time writing letters. I have so many to write, and it isn't very encouraging when you know they are a month old when they get there.

Have you much snow? I haven't seen any yet.

I guess this is all there is to say. I hope you got my cables and airgraph okay.

> Love to all,
> George.

* Riley Hea was a schoolmate of George's at Summerberry, and his father Hartley was their schoolteacher. Riley also flew in Stirlings during the war.

† "Gordons" refers again to the family of George's uncle, Gordon McCowan.

‡ "Uncle Jims" refers to the family of George's uncle, James McCowan, whose son had been killed at No. 11 S.F.T.S. at Yorkton the previous year. The family consisted of James and May McCowan, their deceased son James, and two daughters, Marjorie and Georgina.

§ Robert and Gladys Main farmed near the Kings in the Summerberry district. Their son, Sergeant James Elliott Main, served in the Canadian Army and was killed on 14 August 1944.

LETTER 8.

R142247
SGT. KING G.M.
R.C.A.F. OVERSEAS
January 5th, 1943

Dear Mom, Dad & Bill,

Here I am again. I received an air mail letter from Bill a couple of days ago, and one from Auntie May* the same day. I had just written her the day before. I believe this is about 3 letters within a week I have sent home. It seems every time I write, something comes so I write again.

Bill said in the last letter you had sent 300 cigarettes. I'm glad of that—they will be very welcome as the cigarettes over here are very expensive, and poor when you get them.

Aunt May said in her letter that Stan Sotkowy was missing.† Ken Bourne and I were wondering if he was okay, as he hadn't written either of us for quite some time. I hope he turns up okay. There aren't many better chaps right at the bottom than Stan was, even though people did laugh at him.

I have got a few more hours' flying in, as the weather has been better the last few days. I have 2 more weeks to put in here, and then I go back to where I came from.‡ I like Birmingham very well—I'm going back next week.

I got a letter from Aunt Sally. She says the only thing they can't get they would like is apples. How you could get them to her I don't know. I'd sure like to get to see her. She says that Toms§ were telling her Uncle George has been much better ever since I was to see him. It seemed to cheer him up a lot.

There is another rain storm today—sure lots of it here. There are

---

* "Auntie May" refers to James McCowan's wife, May (Mills) McCowan.

† Stan Sotkowy, the son of Walter and Tillie Sotkowy, was an airman from the Summerberry district.

‡ By this time, George had been posted to No. 9 E.F.T.S. at Ansty, Warwickshire, quite close to Birmingham. He anticipated being sent back to Bournemouth after completing his course.

§ "Toms" refers to Tom King and his family—his mother Daisey, brother Phil, and sister Kathleen.

a lot of these birds they call rooks over here. All I can make out of them are plain crows with an English accent.

I guess it would be quite exciting for the town when the elevator burned.* Do they know how it happened? And are they going to build a new one?

It sure seems to have been cold at home. But I've never been so cold as I am this winter, and I've only seen frost twice.

I have a bit of money ahead right now. If I get any more, I'm going to see if I can send some home. Some say it can't be done, but I'll see. I have to go somewhere there is a Post Office.

The air mail letters seem to work good. It just took about 12 or 13 days for the last one. I can't get hold of any of those forms here so far, but if I do, I'm going to try and get a lot of them. The air mail forms are better than airgraph. You can get quite a bit more in an air mail.

So Doug McMain† is a mystery to the district. If he washed out, why didn't he just admit it? It's no disgrace—lots more have done it. If he can't do it, he just can't. It isn't his fault.

It's too bad about old Snowy‡—she was always my favorite. You say you have 12 loads of wood up—where did you get it? We have a little stove in our hut. It doesn't throw much heat, but it is sure good for toasting bread and then putting this honey on them. It's sure good.

How has the hunting been going? Your shooting must have been red-hot that day, Bill.

How is Dad these days? All I have heard from him for quite a while is a long silence. Uncle George writes me about half a page, but still, it's a letter.

Jim has sure been travelling around down there.§

Poor Aunt May was even talking about Jim** in her letter. It has sure spoiled their lives.

* One of the grain elevators at Summerberry burned down in late 1942.

† Douglas McMain, whose family farmed near the Kings, also served as an airman during the war.

‡ Snowy was one of the King family's cows.

§ Here, George is referring to his brother Jim, stationed in Atlantic Canada.

** Here, George is referring to his cousin Jim, killed on a training flight when his aircraft hit a power line near Yorkton in 1942.

*   Dave Harries was a friend of George's. He and his family, including his brothers Bill, Jack, and Jimmie, farmed near Summerberry on Rod Christie's land.

†   Roy Campbell was another airman from the Summerberry district.

I guess these letters take quite a while to get over. I have written Gordons two, and haven't heard from them yet. Outside of Dave Harries,* they are the only ones I haven't heard from that I have written to.

This is sure a good pen.

I seem to have run right out of news, so I guess I'll close for this time. You have done well writing me letters, so I hope you keep it up.

I forgot to tell you—Roy Campbell† is here now. He came just a week after I did. He seems to stick pretty close to me when he can. None of the other boys are here, so it's sure nice to have Roy here.

Well, I guess this is all.

> Love to all,
> George.

LETTER 9.

R142247
SGT. KING G.M.
R.C.A.F. OVERSEAS
January 13th, 1943

Dear Mother, Dad and Bill,

Well, here I am again. I have just started to receive your air mail letters, and am sure pleased to get them. I have not had any ordinary ones yet, but I have every reason to believe I will tomorrow or the next day. That isn't just a hope, either—the papers say another bunch of Canadians have arrived over here.

I am fine—fat as ever and enjoying myself. I still like England fine, but I would gladly trade a bit of nice, cold, dry snow for this blessed rain.

I imagine you will have some of my mail by now, as it's well over a month since I sent it. Time goes fast, doesn't it? I've been here 6 weeks now.

I haven't been flying yet, and there is no sign of it coming up, either, so I'm just a bit fed up with my easy existence.

I'm glad you had a nice Xmas. Who won the Yule between you and Dad and Mr and Mrs Main this year? I guess Barbara* will be quite the girl now. Her birthday is just a month from today, isn't it?

I can't figure out why the photos are not there from Halifax. They were going to be ready the day after I left. I had paid the $12 and given Holly $3 to send them, so he sure wasn't short of money. Maybe they got held up in the mail. If you don't get them, write to Holly and ask him when he sent them.

Cpl. Hollingshead

R85195 R.C.A.F.

#1 "Y" Depot

Halifax

I guess things will be quite cool at home now. That just sounds like Bill, tearing off to Grenfell to a dance with the wild Harries boys.† I do hope he behaved himself.

Reg Barber‡ made a mistake when he took a navigation course, but they are handing out more commissions since I left, so he has a good chance of getting one, but a bomb aimer is a lot easier, and just as much pay, and as many commissions.

Has Bill done any hunting this year? I guess he will be pretty busy without that, though. How is Dad keeping this winter? I hope he isn't troubled with rheumatism too much.

It was funny about the presents you gave Mac and Joy.§ I read the letter over twice and was thinking it was funny you just said the same

* George's young cousin Barbara McCowan, the daughter of Gordon and Ellen McCowan, was about a year old at the time George wrote this letter.

† "The wild Harries boys"—Bill, Dave, Jack, and Jimmie Harries—were well known in the Summerberry district.

‡ Reg Barber was another airman from the Summerberry district.

§ Mac McCowan was George's uncle, the father of "Young Les." "Joy" refers to the daughter of Agnes' brother, the schoolteacher Les McCowan.

* Bill Smith was the son of Agnes Smith, Agnes King's best friend from Summerberry. He and a number of his brothers—Stuart, Morris, and Rusty—all served in the military during the Second World War.

† Elwood Barber and Eldon Fleming were servicemen whose families farmed in the Summerberry district.

‡ Matt Eagle was a friend of the Kings who farmed near them in the Summerberry district. He died in early 1943.

§ The Landers farmed north of the Kings, and the McMains also had a farm in the district.

as last year and then I remembered the little unmentionables.

I'll be glad to get the pen, as I did buy a good one and then pretty well broke it and they are very hard to get over here. The parcel should be here in a couple of weeks, I think. Things sure come over slow, don't they?

How about the rink this year? Is it going pretty good, [and] is Bill curling?

That was too bad about Bill Smith* having to leave Xmas night, but he was lucky in a way to have Xmas at home. How about the other boys? Were any of them home besides Reg, Elwood, and Eldon?† What about Doug McMain? Where is he now? These questions may be pretty old when you get them, but please answer them because there is no other way to find out.

If I get a 48 I am going to see Aunt Sally. You'd have to go through London to understand how really big it is. It sure takes a lot of getting around in, and when you don't know the place, the little time I was there, it seems to take a fair amount of cash to get around. Of course, this whole country is that way. I could do just as much or more on $2.50 in Canada as I can on a pound over here.

I'm sorry to hear about poor old Matt. I hope it was just for the festive season, and not because he is having a tough time, because that can never do him any good, and poor Mrs Eagle will feel terrible.‡

How are Landers and McMains?§ I hope they are all well.

I seem to have said quite a bit without saying anything. I can't say anything of much interest anyway.

I have been going to a lot of shows, as usual. Uncle George is great for picture shows, but was quite disgusted with the one at Henley when I was there. It was Bambi, one of Walt Disney's shows. He sure talks like Dad. When I wasn't looking at him, it was pretty near like being home. He seems to think a lot the same as Dad does, too. I really got a great kick out of the resemblance. He sure has a lot of good friends there.

I guess I have had my say, so I'll close. Hoping you are all well.

Love,
George.

LETTER 10.

R142247
SGT. KING G.M.
R.C.A.F. OVERSEAS
January 20th, 1943

Dear Mom,

I received three air mail letters from you today, written on Dec. 7th, 12th, and one on Jan. 4th, so they don't seem to be very regular, but some are fast. I am glad you had a nice Xmas. I haven't heard from Jim since Xmas, but got three letters he had written before. I have not received any parcels yet, but it should be here soon. I did not know this airgraph was so good. I will use it more from now on. I hope Dad and Bill are well and that the cold weather isn't bothering you too much. I got an Xmas card from Mr. and Mrs. Eagle today— also Douglas' address. I will write him a letter tomorrow, but I don't know how long it may be till I see him. Hoping you are all well.

Love,
George.

LETTER 11.

R142247
SGT. KING G.M.
R.C.A.F. OVERSEAS
January 23rd, 1943

Dear Mom, Dad and Bill,

Here I am again. I have moved from my first spot,* but am still not doing much. I haven't had any mail from home lately, and this move may hold it up a while. I haven't got the parcels yet, but I guess they will catch up to me.

If this paper seems to have got rather wet, don't think that it took a dunking in the ocean—it just got soaked when my shaving lotion broke in the kit bag coming up here. It smells quite sweet now, but it will probably have lost that when you get it.

I am still with Doug King, but that is the only one of my chums I have left. I have a good chance of getting back with them. I am in with quite a few pilots and bomb aimers, and they are good guys.

I get a day off once a week here, and there is a city fairly close so I can go there.

I got a couple of letters from Jim not so long ago, and he seemed to be enjoying himself. He was at Dartmouth the last one I got.

I guess the weather will be pretty chilly at home now. It isn't really what you could call hot over here, but I haven't seen any snow, not that I'm crazy to as this is plenty cold enough without snow. I think people would freeze over here the way they build fires.

This is an R.A.F. station I am on now, so we eat 4 times a day. That seems a little queer, but I never did kick at eating anyway.

I layed[sic] off for a day, but here I am again. I did a couple of hours' flying yesterday, and this country sure is a lot different from home. There are towns all over the place, and the towns are what we would call cities. It sure felt good to do some flying again.

There is really nothing new to tell you. I hope you are all well at home. How has Dad been this winter? From what I hear, the weather has been cold. I hope it didn't bother his eyes too much. I guess Bill will be kept pretty busy with all the stock, and of course his social activities will keep him quite busy, too.

I wish I had one of T. Eaton's installments, as the lavatories are very short on equipment around here, and newspapers are rather scarce, too.

I don't like to beg, but when you send me a parcel, could you please send some of those shorts? You know—the real fine kind I used to wear? We can't buy anything without coupons here, and we can't get any. Also, some writing paper as I hate this stuff. Outside of sweet things and smokes, I am perfectly happy.

I guess after I have been here for four weeks, I will go back to the same place down south. I guess it is just about the loveliest and free-from-the-war spot in England. It was a millionaires' playground before the war, and they seemed to keep their old prices pretty well, too.*

There are a lot of Aussies and New Zealanders here as well as English students. I like them very well. It was a New Zealander I was flying with, and he is a very nice chap.

I guess this is all for this time. I'll write again soon. Hoping you are all well.

Love to all,
George.

* George was initially stationed at Bournemouth, a former resort town on the south coast of England.

LETTER 12.

R142247
SGT. KING G.M.
R.C.A.F. OVERSEAS
January 28th, 1943

Dear Mom, Dad & Bill,

I just wrote you a couple of days ago, but I am writing again because I recieved[sic] the lovely Waterman set yesterday. It was really good—I needed it, too. I had no pencil at all, and my pen was in bad shape. Thanks very much. I also recieved[sic] the very welcome cigarettes, and they sure taste good. There's nothing quite like the Canadian ones. We got some more Canadian cigarettes today. I don't know just who gave them to us, but they were sent to this station for all the Canadians.*

I'm not doing much. I have done a little flying, more or less to get us used to the English countryside, and it is certainly good training, because it sure is a lot different from Canada. It's rather nice to do some flying again. I have been flying with New Zealanders and Aussies here—they are nice chaps.

I can't get airgraph from here, but I think I may be able to get one of those blue air letters a week, so I can send one of those.

I got a letter from Uncle George today. He said to give his best to you when I wrote. I haven't managed to see Aunt Sally yet, but I should be able to in about 2 more months if I don't get a 48 before then. Aunt Daisy wrote me a letter a few days ago.

I am having an awful time trying to write letters these days, as there never is anything to write about. There is a picture show here tomorrow nite—"Santa Fe Trail." I saw it in Grenfell about 2 yrs. ago,

* During the war there were a number of programs in place to send cigarettes to overseas servicemen, and this shipment must have been the result of one of these initiatives.

45

but it was a good show, so I think I will go again.

There is a lot of fog around here, and lots of rain and mud. I much prefer the good dry cold of old Sask., of course when people never have anything else to kick at, they kick at the weather, as Podge says. By the way, how are him and Betty making out? Has he still got his job at Regina Industries?

Tom King sure has a great memory—he was asking about all the horses we had when he was there and all the neighbors. He sure seemed to love animals. I guess that's a weakness of the family.

Is Bill doing any trapping this winter? You said in the last letter he had some rabbits. I would like to do a bit of hunting myself. There are lots of Hun[garian] partridges around here—I often wish for a shotgun. We get a day off every Tues. I think I'll go into Birmingham next Tues.

I don't know just what I was begging for in the last letter, but if you could send me a tin of pipe tobbacco[sic] it would really be okay.

I'm sorry I can't make a more interesting letter, but I will keep writing anyway.

How are Uncle Jims, Gordons, Mains, McMains, and Landers? Remember me to them all.

Don't tell Mrs. McMain if she thinks it is rather smart for Doug to have been chasing cattle, but the Air Force considers that very foolish and nothing smart about it. It isn't in the training, and as they say, he will get ample chance to show his daring when the time comes.

I guess that's all for this time. Thanks very much for the nice presents.

Love to all,
George.

LETTER 13.

R142247
SGT. KING G.M.
R.C.A.F. OVERSEAS
January 31st, 1943

Dear Mom, Dad & Bill,

Here I am again. I received the box of cakes, shortbread, date cake and all yesterday and did it ever taste good—or I'd better say does it ever taste good, as there is still lots left. I sure did a good job on the shortbread. I haven't tasted anything like that for months. Just like being at home. The parcel carried very well. The ginger snaps took a bit of a beating, but they are still good. I haven't opened the fruit cake yet, or had any honey yet, but everything else has been sampled, and as Simm said, it sure hits the spot. The choc[o]late bars are sure something new over here.

I told you in a letter a couple of days ago that I had received the pen and pencil set and the fags. It is sure a swell set. The pen is working right now, and sure works fine. Did I tell you what happened to the good pen I bought at Halifax? Well, one of my first nites in this country in the blackout I tangled with a lamp post. The pen, being in my breast pocket, got a rather hard crack and hasn't been working so well lately. I had often seen cartoons of drunks draped around lamp posts, but it was no fun being dead sober and wrapped around one. They have a habit of setting the lamp posts in the middle of the streets here.

I haven't done much flying since I came here. There has been a lot of rain and fog. We wear long rubbers around this station a lot of the time, and we really need to.

I wrote a letter to Uncle George and one to Aunt Sally yesterday. I find it a lot easier to write Uncle George since I have met him. I'm sure he was glad to have me. He even said in his last letter he was lonesome after I left.

I haven't been able to get an air mail form yet, but I will one of these days.

Where did Montys go from Summerberry? Is it a step up the ladder for Monty? They'll miss the old girl with her queer mixture of good and bad points. In fact, I think Summerberry has lost one of its greatest characters of the 20th century. From what you say, this new bird takes things very easy. Is he married? Any family?*

The air mail letters are really fine, but will one member of the family sit down and write me an ordinary letter, a sort of little newspaper giving me all the dope on the district? They come pretty nearly as fast as some of the air mail. Others of the air mail come much faster.

I guess things are going pretty slow for air crews over here. It looks as though it will be several months before I get anywhere near the Huns.† I know what you think about that, Mom, but I'm not just the same.

I guess it's about time for dinner, so I'll finish this later. (Rice pudding for des[s]ert. I ate shortbread instead.)

There is one of the officers here—an instructor—and I am disappointed every time he opens his mouth. He looks so much like Bill Harries I expect him to talk like him. He has the same way of sort of squinting at you like Bill does, too. I'll bet he's Welsh. He was the first person I flew with over here, and he is a real nice chap.

It's nice that Jim got to those people's place for Xmas. I got a letter from him and he seemed to enjoy himself pretty well there.

*   Mr Montgomery, known locally as "Monty," operated the railway station at Summerberry.

†   "Huns" was a World War I era term for "Germans," and was still in use in World War II.

48

I haven't written to Douglas Irons* yet, but I will pretty soon. I guess it was Jim that used to go around with him.

Jeannie was going to give me Nell Bigg's address, but she seems to have forgotten, but there always seems[sic] to be more people than you can get to see, anyway. Aunt Dais has given me Phil's† address in London, and I haven't been able to get to see Aunt Sally yet, and that is the most important thing for me right now. Aunt Dais said Aunt Sally is still very bright, but Lottie is not so good. She is quite feeble and her mind wanders a lot.

Since I have come out here, I am not having much trouble with English money not hanging out. There is nowhere to spend it, so I guess I'll save a bit. In a city, it is very difficult to save any money at all. Ken Bourne is sure sending home a lot of money. Half of my chums are sending $18 a month home, and very few are sending as much as $30. I think I may be able to send home more later on, or put some in the bank over here. But I would sooner have any surplus sent home. I don't know if you can send money home directly, but I will see the next time I get to somewhere there is a Post Office.

I guess this is about all I have to say for this time. I hope you are all well at home, and thanks again for the present and the swell box of cakes. It must have been hard work making all that, and very hard on the sugar ration also. You are really too good to me.

Love,
George.

49

LETTER 14.

R142247
SGT. KING G.M.
R.C.A.F. OVERSEAS
February 11th, 1943

Dear Folks,

I have managed to get a form for an air letter at last, so I hope you get it quick. I had a letter from Jim yesterday, but haven't had any from you in a long while. I suppose you will have got letters from me saying I had received the pen and pencil, cigarettes, and box. They were sure a swell lot of presents. The pen and pencil really are good. This is the pen doing the writing right now. The cigarettes were really a nice change—I don't care for these. But that parcel …I hadn't tasted anything like that since I left home, and you managed to send me so much, and it came over good—everything was nice and fresh. The shortbread was really great.

I seem to get more letters from Jim than anyone. The last one I got from him came over by boat and only took 3 wks. He was at Cape Breton and seemed to like it very well. I had a letter from Aunt May. She was at Winnipeg when she wrote it. Poor soul seemed to say so much about Jim. I'll never get over being sorry for them.*

I guess I told you Roy Campbell is here too. We always go out together—he is really a fine chap. I will be leaving a week before him, but he will follow me in a wk.

You will probably hear about German raids over the radio and see it in the papers, but that's as far as I've got myself. I have yet to see a German aircraft. That seems rather funny.

I guess winter will be losing its sting by the time you get this letter.

* The "Jim" mentioned here is George's cousin, James Gordon McCowan, who had been killed while training at Yorkton in May of 1942. In this passage, George expresses sympathy for Jim's parents, May and James McCowan.

I hope that cold weather didn't last too long.

I hope I'm not writing so small you can't read this, because I'm afraid I won't be able to fill all the space.

I like the midlands where I am now better than the south coast. People are much more friendly up here. I can truthfully say I like it up here and I like the people. It was a rather high-class summer resort where I was before—in fact it was the summer resort of England—and as long as you kept paying through the nose, they were quite happy.

I may get a little leave after I'm through here, so I will be able to see Aunt Sally, so that will be nice.

Are Aunt Mamie and Jim still at Summerberry? I wonder what is the matter with Gordon's—I have written them, but still have no letters. Maybe they haven't got them yet.

How is the hunting coming now, Bill? I guess you probably will have all the Jacks cleared out by now. I wouldn't mind having the .22 here—all these rooks around here would sure make good shooting.

I guess it's getting about time for my fourth meal of the day. I'm getting used to eating all these meals—of course, they aren't all good squares like we get at home.

This seems to be about all there is to say for this time. I think I may get one or two more of these forms before I leave here.

Love to all,
George.

LETTER 15.

R142247
SGT. KING G.M.
R.C.A.F. OVERSEAS
February 19th, 1943

Dear Mom,

Here I am again, back where I can get an airgraph from.* I think I'll try quite a few of them, as I can see by your last letter my third or fourth was the first one you got. I got the ordinary letter you sent me, and was sure pleased to get it. There is more room in them. I don't know just how many of my letters you are getting, but I have written more than one a week in the last four weeks. I have written six as well as one air mail. I have received your Xmas parcel and the pen and pencil set, and Bill's cigarettes. I got 300 cigarettes from Jim a couple of days ago, but that is all that has got here so far, and from your letters I think some more should be here by now. I haven't managed to see Aunt Sally just yet, but the first leave I get, I will. I hope it isn't too cold at home just now, and you are all well. I'll write a longer letter in a day or two.

Love to all,
George.

* By this time, George had returned to Bournemouth to await a further posting.

LETTER 16.

R142247
SGT. KING G.M.
R.C.A.F. OVERSEAS
February 25th, 1943

Dear Mom, Dad & Bill,

Here I am again, right on time with my letter—a day or two ahead of a wk., in fact. I have received no mail at all from home in a week. No air mail for over two wks., so I should get a pile one of these days. I doubt if you are getting mine very well, as you keep asking me things I have told you months ago.

Mrs Sitter is in her usual form of a long deep silence. I finally did hear from Norma and Jean and Dave Harries. I had pretty nearly given them up as a bad job.

I got a letter from Buck Fisher yesterday. He will soon be back with me again. I am with most of the old gang now. I ran into Ralph Fleming again the other nite. He seems to be doing fine. It was nice to see him.

I got the last letter I wrote to Stan Sotkowy back. From what I could make out of the postmarks and the marks they put on it, my letter was four days late. That's sure a shame about Stan. I hope he is alright.*

I'm doing nothing again—it gets pretty tiresome. I'd like to get back to work.

I haven't received any more parcels since your two Xmas ones— that is, the pen set and box and cigarettes. I got some cigarettes Jim sent me, but none of the other boxes. I'm beginning to think Davey Jones has been at some of them.† It's rather too bad when people go

* Stan Sotkowy, a friend of George's from the Summerberry area, was killed in action on December 17, 1942. When he writes this letter, George is aware only that Stan has been reported missing in action. By the time he writes the letter of April 1, however, George has learned that Stan has been killed.

† "Davy Jones" was an 18th and 19th-century slang term for what sailors believed to be the malevolent spirit of the sea. "Davy Jones's locker" referred to the bottom of the ocean, the resting-place of those who perish at sea. By saying that "Davey Jones has been at some of" his letters, George means that German predation of Atlantic shipping may have sunk ships that were bringing his letters to Canada. Because he suspects that many of his letters are not getting to Canada, he tends to repeat himself in his letters home.

to all the trouble—not to mention the poor sailors. Speaking of sailors, I wasn't seasick on the way over, but give me the air any day.

How is everyone at home? How did Bill's hunting go this year? How has Dad been this winter? I guess the cold weather would make him rather stiff. And what about you, Mom? I hope you are taking care of yourself.

It's too bad about the rink not going so good this year—it was about all the town had to keep it alive during the winter.

Has Dave Harries got back from the Army yet? That would sure go tough on Bill. Even with all his energy, that's just too much for one man.

I hear from Ken Bourne quite regularly. He seems to be doing okay. I get a letter from Riley and Lawrence every so often. I still haven't written to Douglas Irons and Phil King. I guess I had better soon snap out of it.

The weather is really turning very nice here now. There are some trees in blossom. I haven't found out just what they are yet, but it is a pink blossom and I'm suspicious of apples. Apples! That reminds me of cackle berries. I haven't seen one in months. Remember me and two fried eggs for breakfast every morning? I'm still not losing weight, though.

I guess this is all I have room for this time, so I'll say so-long.

Love to all,
George.

LETTER 17.

R142247
SGT. KING G.M.
R.C.A.F. OVERSEAS
March 11th, 1943

Dear Mom,

Just a quick letter to let you know I have received the box for my birthday and it came over fine, and such a lot in it. I wrote you a long letter yesterday telling you I had received it, but I got this form today so I thought I would write again quick. They try to give us one of these forms each a wk., but they don't always manage it. I got an air letter from you just a few minutes ago. It was written on the 24th of Feb.

I'm doing very well for parcels. I got your Xmas one as well as the pen and pencil set and Bill's cigarettes. Now I have had Ellen's and Aunt Annie's and now your birthday one in the last three days—also 300 cigs. from you, the H.M.'s,* and Jim, so I seem to be far from forgotten. I guess I've told you I'm back on the ground waiting again. It was nice to do some flying again, anyway. You said in the last letter you had sent the shorts and writing paper. I'll sure be pleased to get the shorts.

I did send you a little private letter one time, Mom. Well don't bother about it if you haven't because I've fixed that up myself. Of course you can tell me what you think.†

I still claim the two quietest people in the world are Mrs. F.B. Sitter and her Father. It wouldn't hurt for Bill to drop me a line one of these days, as he will be pretty busy in a little while. I have written Aunt May at least twice since I had the honey, Mother. These choc.

* The Summerberry Homemakers' Club had sent George 300 cigarettes.

† The "private letter" to which George refers probably made arrangements to buy his father a birthday present, as William's birthday was April 5th.

55

bars and gum are sure good. We do get a very small allowance of choc[o]late but never see gum. I told you I was enclosing Aunt Sally's letter in this last one. Well after I posted it I found Aunt Sally's still here, so you see my mind has not improved any. Auntie says she will write to you as soon as she has seen me. Fisher will be back with us in a week. All the rest of the old gang are here. The weather is lovely and we really have a good time.

So Bill drove into Grenfell with Harry and Daisy? Just what does he mean, breaking up that team of mine, Beaut and Harry? Oh well, I can still say all Beaut knows about threshing and wood hauling I taught her, and as for Daisy, I taught her all she knows—at least all the good she knows.*

I guess this is all I have room for this time. I'll write again soon.

> Your loving son,
> George.

* Harry, Daisy, and Beaut—as well as Doc, who is mentioned later—were all workhorses on the farm. (Doc and Daisy are featured in the above photo, circa 1932).

LETTER 18.

> R142247
> SGT. KING G.M.
> R.C.A.F. OVERSEAS
> April 1st, 1943

Dear Mom, Dad & Bill,

Here comes my week's issue of air letters. I hope you are all well—personally, I'm in the pink. I haven't had much mail from you lately. One air letter in seven weeks I believe is the grand total. The big surprise is over half the mail I am getting these days is from Jeannie. It is sure a great change. I got 2 air letters from her and a birthday card and letter today. One air letter from Aunt May and one from Norma and Jean. That is the first overseas mail I have had for about 7 or 8 weeks except Dad's air letter. Nothing at all from Jim for ages, so I don't suppose anyone has heard from me much either even though I have been writing.

Things are very much the same here as they have been. I'm still pretty much unemployed. I guess I told you last week Ken Bourne was down to see me for three days. It was sure great to see him. He seems quite happy and is really looking fine. I wrote Bob MacFarlane[sic]* a letter and got it sent back to me. They said they had sent it to his unit and to other units but there was no record of him so I don't know just what to think. Fisher is an officer now. They sent three of my class commissions over here. Fisher and Campbell both got one. They really deserved them before—especially Fisher. I'm afraid poor Buck is a bit lost in his new place—he is around to see me every night. He never misses. It sure didn't change Buck any.

I guess things will be getting pretty busy around home now. You will be starting to work on the land in about 3 wks. It would be sort of nice to be home to work for a few days. Jim said the same thing in his last letter to me. I guess nothing will ever take all of the farming out of a person's blood. Take that storekeeper at home. After he had been back home about 12 hrs he was giving the barn a going over.

I see in the papers wheat is up to a dollar a bus[hel]. How is it for selling? Can you sell all you want to?

That's sure sad about Stan Sotkowy, but he did all he could and Stan was proud to do it.†

I'm glad everyone got the pictures. I have heard from Aunt May and Norma and Jean and Jeannie. They all said they were okay, but that is only natural. I hope they were alright.

* Bob McFarlane was a friend of George's from the Summerberry area, whose family had also lived at Peebles.

† By this time, George knows that Stan Sotkowy is not simply missing, but has been killed in action.

How are the Landers and McMains these days? I guess Edwin* will be getting his tractor in running order.

I guess this is all for now.

Love to all,
George.

LETTER 19.

R142247
SGT. KING G.M.
R.C.A.F. OVERSEAS
April 1st, 1943

Dear Jim,

Well here it is again. I have heard nowt from you for two months now but I know you are writing. At least you'd better be or you'll have my 180 of bones and muscle right in the basket.

Except for Jeannie I would hardly get any mail. It really jars me to think of her writing so much.

I don't know whether I told you I had been up to London to see Aunt Sally. She is really wonderful for her age. Ken Bourne had some leave and came down here to see me for three days. We really had a great time, got a bit woozy all three nights, and really talked over old times and covered the district in general.

How are things in the east? The St John's queen, etc.?† I don't just know how things are for me, but I think I'm just about washed up with P.K.‡ It won't make me have a guilty conscience anymore.

This isn't much. A big one will follow.

Love,
George.

* Edwin McMain was the eldest son of the McMain family, and ran the family farm near the Kings' farm.

Jim King on the banks of the Assiniboine River, circa 1942.

† By "queen," George means "woman," and so it seems that he is asking his brother James about a woman from St John's, Newfoundland—or, if his spelling is incorrect, St John, New Brunswick.

‡ "P.K." refers to Patsy Kerr, George's girlfriend.

LETTER 20.

R142247
SGT. KING G.M.
R.C.A.F. OVERSEAS
April 5th, 1943

Dear Mom,

I wrote an air letter a couple of days ago but I guess another letter now won't hurt anything. There isn't much to tell—everything is much the same as usual. I got quite a bit of mail last week and I wasn't sorry for that as I haven't had much lately. I guess things will be getting pretty busy around home now. I hope Dad has a good birthday. I am sending a telegram but I'm afraid something has turned up that will make it late. Fisher is here getting some air graphs written too, and Doug King is just an onlooker. Doug comes from Pontrilas, Sask. That's near Nipiwan[sic]. There are a lot of Sask. men here. His Dad is the King that you have read about in the wheat competitions.

It was sure nice seeing Aunt Sally—she is really wonderful. I'm pretty proud of her. Dad sure would be if he could see her.

Love,
George.

LETTER 21.

R142247
SGT. KING G.M.
R.C.A.F. OVERSEAS
April 16th, 1943

Dear Mom, Dad & Bill,

Well, here I am again. I've made another move.* It is a bit of a lonesome spot, but it doesn't bother [me] because there are ten of us came from the other place up here together, and they are all really nice chaps. I've been with them all since I came to England. Doug King is here. Dick Boulter is the only one from Pearce that came up here. The rest of the old gang are spread all over.

We have to work pretty hard, and longer hours than I've ever worked since I've been in the air force. We are going to do a lot of flying in a little while, so it will be a good change.

I got a letter from Fisher today. He seems to be doing okay. I got four letters from Canada last week. One from you and Bill, Jim, Jeannie, and my old faithful at Regina.† She never misses. Nice to get, too.

I'm back in the midlands again, so I guess I may get into Birm. again. We do get a day off each week, but I don't think I will make Birmingham.

Their[sic] is one of the boys here [who] has a little gramophone, and we really enjoy it.

I guess something has happened to the Homemakers' box, some of Jeannie's, and my shorts. They haven't got here, and they have been on the way for to[sic] long not to have been here. Verda's‡ cigarettes, too. I am out of cigarettes just now. I have been for a while.

There was a Canadian Padre here today.§ He had a talk with the

* By this time, George had been posted to No. 3 Advanced Flying Unit, based out of Bobbington, Staffordshire.

† By this time, Patsy had moved from Summerberry to Regina, where she lived at 285 Angus Crescent.

‡ Verda was the wife of Agnes' brother Les McCowan, and therefore was George's aunt.

§ The "Canadian Padre" may have been Squadron Leader W.J. Bell, the chaplain from Lloydminster who would later conduct George's funeral service and write two heartfelt letters of condolence to George's parents.

Canadian boys. He was really nice, and he talked in the right way to make a person feel pretty good.

Uncle Jim is going to be pretty busy working the old farm. Is all that good pasture going to go to waste? That is one farm that was never meant to be just a tractor farm. The people up here are just the same as the last time I was up in this country—very friendly.

I hear quite regularly from Uncle George and Aunt Sally. They are both fine.

I was thinking about you yesterday, Dad. I hope you had a good birthday and that you got my telegram. Just when I was going to send it, some new boys came in and I didn't want my telegram mixed with theirs, as they are always held back a bit, so I'm afraid yours would be late. But I hope you enjoyed it. Remember when you and I used to amalgamate* and Mom cooked up the cream puffs? I always walked off the bloated lad.

I guess this is all I have room for, so I hope your[sic] all fine.

> Love to all,
> George.

LETTER 22.

> C.N. Telegraphs
> R142247
> SGT. KING G.M.
> R.C.A.F. OVERSEAS
> April 19th, 1943

Mr. Wm. King, Summerberry Sask.,

Many happy returns. Best wishes.

George King.†

* George's birthday was 19 April, and his father's was 5 April.

† This telegram was in response to a birthday telegram George had just received from his family.

61

LETTER 23.

R142247
SGT. KING G.M.
R.C.A.F. OVERSEAS
April 23rd, 1943

Dear Mom, Dad & Bill,

I guess it's time I was sending you another letter. It's just about a week since I sent the last one.

I had a great birthday, as I got four letters and my shorts and a parcel from Jeannie. Then I got another from Jeannie the next day, too. I got 12 letters today. Three of them from Jeannie, two from home with lots of clippings from the "Sun."* Thelma† sent me an Easter card—it was really good. Also a letter and a photo of her and another teacher. Also one of Bruce going into the store. I got a letter from Ellen and a photo of Barbara.‡ She is really cute and such a pretty little girl. I sure wish I could see her now. I got a letter from Mrs Main the other day. It was really a nice letter.

The shorts were fine, Mom, just what I wanted. I was sure pleased to get them.

That is certainly a shame about Mr Eagle. It is hard to realize, isn't it? Matt was always such a big, healthy man. It is so sorry for Mrs Eagle—she will be so much alone. He is all she has.

I hope you got the letter telling you to take $10 out for Dad's birthday§—also that Dad got the wire.

I guess Eldon has his wings by now. Noreen** even wrote me a letter and the main purpose seemed to be to inform me of the coming event. Oh well, it is nice to get them. The novelty wears off fairly fast, but it is always something a person is proud of, anyway.

I guess I told you before that I am back up in the Midlands and

* The "Sun" refers to the Grenfell Sun newspaper.

† Thelma Evans was a family friend who taught school near Kindersley.

‡ Ellen McCowan was George's aunt, and Barbara, her daughter, was his one-year-old cousin.

§ $10 in 1943 would be roughly $112 in today's currency.

** Noreen Fleming was Eldon's sister.

* At the time, George was posted to No. 3 A.F.U. in Bobbington, Staffordshire.

† George flew in Avro Anson light bombers during A.O.S. in Canada at Pearce and Regina, and that is the aircraft he was training in at A.F.U. in Bobbington at the time he wrote this letter. At other points in his RCAF career, he also flew in de Havilland Tiger Moth training aircraft during E.F.T.S. at Ansty, in Vickers Wellington "Wimpy" bombers during O.T.U. at Hixon, and in Stirlings as part of a Conversion Unit at Waterbeach and during operations based out of Downham Market.

navigating again.* I rather enjoy it—it is rather nice to get flying again and to get back to work, and we really do work and when we fly we really do that too. Two times in a day. They are in the same kind of aircraft as I flew in at Pearce and Regina.† I still have quite a bit of training to do before I'm ready for anything. I must say, they really make sure a person knows their stuff before they get doing anything.

I got a letter from Aunt Dais today. She wants to know when I'm coming on leave again. She says my bed is airing for me, just waiting till I get there. They are all fine. Uncle George has had a cold, but he is better now.

I got some cigarettes from Jim and some from Aunt Georgie a couple of days ago, so you see I am going nearly mad trying to answer all these letters and parcels. Jeannie's parcels were really dandies—everything you could imagine.

I seem to be out of news for this time. I'll write again as soon as I can.

> Love to all,
> George.

LETTER 24.

> R142247
> SGT. KING G.M.
> R.C.A.F. OVERSEAS
> May 1st, 1943

Dear Mom, Dad & Bill,

I guess it is about time I was sending another letter. I have been writing very regularly lately, averaging about 2 per week.

This is our day off today, so I have lots of time to write. There isn't anywhere to go in the daytime anyway. There is a little town here and always a dance there at night. We went to one last nite and may go again tonite, and then it's work for another week. We just have a little over a week left on our course here, and then we go on to more advanced training in bigger aircraft. I'll be glad when I get doing that—it will make it more interesting. We get a crew there, too.

We do quite a bit of P.T.* here. They had us out for a cross-country run yesterday, and I think the doggoned instructor used to be a marathon runner. My tongue was hanging right down to the ground when I finished, but it is good to get out and get some exercise.

There are some things I would like you to send me—some fine socks and a silver grey shirt. Take the money out of what I send home. I have some money here now, but I will be getting leave and I'd like to have some to spare then.

I hope you get the flowers and the cable for Mother's Day, Mom. There isn't much you can say in a cable, but you know what I mean by them.

I've sure had a lot of parcels lately. Aunt Lizzie and Aunt Georgie† both sent one. I got yours with the socks in it. The socks are fine. Aunt Lizzie sent a pair, too, so as far as heavy socks go, I'm really well-fixed.

Jeannie is sure writing me lots of letters and sending lots—I have her two parcels now. I got an Easter card and letter from Thelma Evans. It was a real nice letter, sort of the same type as Gladys Taylor‡ used to write. I have sure been writing a lot lately [what with] all the letters and parcels I have got. Pat sent me a box of nuts. They are something you never get over here.

I guess this is all I have to say for this time—there isn't much news, really. I hope you are all well. I guess you will be pretty busy now. How is Uncle Jim making out with his two farms?

> Love to all,
> George.

*   "P.T." refers to physical training.

†   Georgie (McCowan) Mills was Agnes' sister who lived in Winnipeg. Lizzie was the wife of Agnes' brother, David McCowan.

‡   Gladys Taylor was a relative of George's aunt, Annie (McCowan) Taylor. Annie was married to Ernest Taylor and lived at Pinkham.

LETTER 25.

R142247
SGT. KING G.M.
R.C.A.F. OVERSEAS
May 8th, 1943

Dear Mom, Dad & Bill,

Just about time for me to rear my head again with my weekly news—not much news, either.

Things are going much the same with me. I am leaving this station in a few days now. I'm going to get on bigger aircraft now, so that should be interesting. I was supposed to fly tonite, but it is raining cats and dogs just now, so I guess we won't. There hasn't been much rain here lately, but it has made up for it today.

I haven't been having much mail lately, just that air letter from Dad telling me he got the cable. I sure hope you get the cable and flowers on time for tomorrow, Mom. They told me they would, so I hope there is someone down to the train tonite because they will probably be on it.

That was sure good news about Tunis this morning.* It looks as though there should be something popping pretty soon, at least. According to my strategy, they would clean up Africa before they did anything else—of course, I won't boast about my strategy.

I got a letter from Riley yesterday. He went down to that place I was at before I came here† and just missed me by one day. It would have been nice to see Riley, but I was really fed up with that place, and was pleased to get out and get flying again.

I guess there will be lots of work these days with all the cows and the work besides on the land. Bill has turned out to be quite a genius,

* Tunis fell on 7 May 1943, near the end of the North African campaign.

† George is referring to the Canadian holding depot at Bournemouth, where he spent a fair amount of time awaiting postings to other units.

65

putting two and two together with the implements. How is Howard making out with the spring work? Has he still got the same horses? I guess you will have your leghorns by now, Mom. It's too bad about the reds—they are really good all round.

What about old Major?* Does he still charge around in his rough fashion? He is getting quite old now.

I thought maybe I would be getting back to Henley and to London when I finished this course, but we are going straight onto the next course. They really give you good training here.

This is really man-sized writing paper—Jeannie sent me this. It is really an accomplishment to fill these pages.

I guess Edwin will really be going big-time on the tractor these days.

It sort of surprised me when I heard George Hollingshead† had joined up. Poor Mrs Hollingshead doesn't seem to have anyone to stay with her.

I got another letter from Bill. He seems to have really cooked up a real yarn if it isn't the truth about those pictures.

Well, I guess this is about all I have to say for this time, so I guess I may as well close for this time. Hoping you are all well.

> Love to all,
> George.

* Major was the family dog.

† George Hollingshead, whose family farmed near the Kings, was the brother of Bill Hollingshead, the serviceman who was supposed to send George's pictures home, but had not done so by this time.

The King family on the farm, circa 1935. Left to right, Agnes, Georgie Mills, William, George, Jim, Bill, and Joe Mills. In front: Major.

LETTER 26.

R142247
SGT. KING G.M.
R.C.A.F. OVERSEAS
May 10th, 1943

Dear Mom,

Here it is again—I've made a move since I wrote last.* We just got here today, but it looks as though it would be okay.

There were some Canadian pilots came in today too, and who is the first one I meet but Norm Spencer, the chap I did my flying with in Jan. and Feb.? So we were both tickled pink, to say the least. I am still with the boys I was [with] at the last place, so I have lots of nice friends.

Things are still much the same. I haven't been able to get out to see Aunt Sally or Uncle George since the first time I saw them. The last letter I had from Aunt Dais, some of them were going up to London to see Aunt Sally, so I guess she would be pretty pleased. She really likes company.

This paper I am writing on was given to us by the club in Canada. We got 50 cigarettes and the writing paper and envelopes. They were rather nice to get, even though I have lots of writing paper.

I guess you will really be busy these days. This place sort of puts me in mind of home. There are cows out in the pasture right behind our hut. It is sort of nice to see them around.

I'm getting pretty tired now, so I guess I'll finish this tomorrow.

Well, I guess I can finish this now. Still nothing to say, but the food is first-class on this station. We do have to get up in the morning, a habit I have sort of got out of lately.

* At this point, George had just been posted to No. 30 O.T.U. at Hixon, Staffordshire.

That was certainly too bad about Mr Eagle—the last man you would have thought it of, too. He seemed so healthy. Poor Mrs Eagle—what will she do now?

We have a Sgt.'s mess here and get served and everything else.

We haven't had any leave since Xmas and I don't believe we will for quite a time yet now that we are here. I have got quite a bit saved up right now, and should be able to have a nice time with Uncle George when I get there.

We start working tomorrow, and from what I've heard, you really do work—and hard, too—but that suits me okay. I don't mind that like I do sitting around doing nothing at all.

I guess I have had everything that has been sent to me, except the Homemakers' box and Verda's cigarettes. At the last station I had 4 boxes all lined up on the shelf and all the other boys had them too, so we had a heck of a time getting everything cleaned up, but we did in the end.

I guess this is all for this time. I seem to be right out of news, more or less because there is none.

I hope you are all well at home.

Love to all,
George.

LETTER 27.

R142247
SGT. KING G.M.
R.C.A.F. OVERSEAS
May 19th, 1943

Dear Mom,

Here goes a day or two ahead of time, but I got an air mail from you yesterday and was really pleased to get it as I was a little worried about the flowers getting there on time, and it really pleased me to hear they did. The letter came in 8 days, so the news was still red-hot.

I guess Uncle Jims would feel rather bad on Mother's Day.* I guess they feel rather bad quite often. It seems rather funny Johnnie Slabiak† and Jim were such good pals.

What is all this about Sgt. Pilot Lawrence Brierly?‡ The last I heard of him he was a Corp. Aero Engine mech[anic]. I also got a surprise when you said Reg Barber got a commission. I expected to hear that of Red Fleming§ before Reg Barber. Reg should have got one anyway because he would have a lot of training on that on his pilot's course before he ever had to go to A.O.S.** and practice is the whole thing in my opinion. But I'm sure Red Fleming would get one too.

I'm glad to hear Jim is getting his tooth fixed—it certainly took them a long time to get around to it.

You were asking did I ever hear from Riley. Well, I do about once every 6 wks. He seems to enjoy himself very well, but he just missed me at that place I was at when I saw Ralph Fleming and Ken Bourne. I left one day and Riley got there the next, so that brought a letter from him.

There are four Canadians and one Welshman in our crew. Two

* As noted before, their son had been killed on a training flight at No. 11 S.F.T.S., Yorkton, on May 11, 1942.

† Johnnie Slabiak was another airman from the Summerberry district who was killed in the war.

‡ Lawrence Brierly was another airman from the Summerberry area.

§ Red Fleming was from one of the Fleming families near Summerberry.

** "A.O.S." stands for "Air Observer School," which George had attended at Regina and at Pearce.

Toronto men and one from Vancouver. You have heard of this Vancouver man before—Norm Spencer, the same pilot I did all the flying with last winter. The Bomb Aimer and A.G.* (Doug Wylie and Bill Baker) are the other two, both very nice chaps. The one lone Welshman† seems to be quite happy about it. He is a Wireless Op—a short, fair-haired little guy and always seems happy about everything. They are as good a bunch as I've ever been around, but you wouldn't know just how pleased I was when I saw Spencer turn up here.

I believe I had the lowest trick played on me the other night I ever had in my life. I wrote a letter to Joe,‡ stamped it, addressed it, and put it in my pad. I was going to post it on the way back to my hut. I just set the pad down on a window sill while I got a sandwich. Well, I was gone about 3 minutes, came back, and the pad was stolen. I wrote Joe another letter last night so if the thief has a small twinge of conscience, Joe will get two letters in pretty hot succession.

I can't get any of those blue air letters to send at all. They aren't used much, as they don't have as many Canadians here. I did get all your parcels, shorts, and socks the next time and everything was just fine. The shortbread was really swell. It's a funny thing, but I have never met a fellow that doesn't like shortbread. I can't understand anyone not [liking it], but in our family there were some, weren't there? I got all the tobacco, too. You are sure good to me—it must be a lot of trouble to you.

What is Grenfell doing about its glorious 24th§ this year? Things should be quite in a dither around there just now.

I wrote both Uncle George and Aunt Sally the other night, so I will be getting a letter from Aunt Sally pretty soon. Uncle George will send one in a couple of weeks, anyway. When I write to Aunt Dais, I always get quite a prompt answer, too. The last letter I got from her,

* "A.G." stands for "Air Gunner.

† Harold "Taffy" Hicks, of Cardiff, Wales, was the Wireless Operator in George's crew. At the time he was killed, he had a two-year-old son named Raymond.

‡ Joe Mills was George's cousin from Winnipeg, the son of Agnes' sister Georgie Mills.

§ Grenfell's "glorious 24th" refers to Victoria Day celebrations, which before 1952 were held on the actual date of Queen Victoria's birthday, May 24.

she said my bed was just airing waiting for my next leave. I hope it doesn't have to wait long is all I can say. They sure treated me nice there. It really made Xmas like Xmas for me.

I guess Bill and his ingenious implements will be all through with the oats and going to work on the fallow by the time you get this. I guess you will all be busy these days. How is Dad making out with his garden? I wish I could see it and the house now [that] you have the new paper up. I guess it will look different. Do you like it?

This seems to be all for this time, so I guess I will close for now. Hoping you are all well.

> Your loving son,
> George.

P.S. Don't use #3 P.A.C. for an address for me anymore. That has been out of date for some time now. G.M.K.

LETTER 28.

> R142247
> SGT. KING G.M.
> R.C.A.F. OVERSEAS
> May 27th, 1943

Dear Mom, Dad & Bill,

I received 2 very welcome letters from you today. The one was all Mother's, and one from Mom and Bill. I was really pleased to get them, as it is quite a while since I've had any.

I guess I have to quit—they are going to play ball and want me to come and pitch.

Okay, so I went to pitch and the other team didn't show up, so it took exactly 45 minutes of my valuable time for nothing. As a general rule, my time isn't valuable, but I got eight letters today and want to answer them. There were 2 from you, 2 from Jeannie, three from Jim, and Davey Harries wrote me again. Dave's letter took a little over 2 months to get here. It sure seems funny—the end of May, and Dave was talking about the Carnival at Grenfell and the curling at home.

How about Jack and Jim Harries? Did either of them have to go into the Army? I didn't think Jimmie would pass a medical after being sick like he was.

Red Fleming is lucky to be going down east to fly—that sounds like O.T.U.* in Canada. It really isn't a very useful course, but it does put you in a nice type of aircraft when you come over here. Unless it puts him Coastal Command—that is pretty dull.

I got a letter from Aunt Sally a couple of days ago. She is fine. I wrote to Uncle George the same time, but I haven't got an answer from him yet. He always takes lots of time answering a letter.

I got a letter from Fisher today. He is about a month behind me as far as training over here goes. He is with two of the boys that were at Pearce with us (Rand and Thorn).

I am going to have some pictures of the crew to send home to you. We have a few now, but we took some more the other day. I think they should be pretty good.

We had a day off yesterday and went in to Birmingham and had a pretty good time. They had a big tent there with a dance in it, but it closed at 9 o'clock and we didn't get there until 8, so we didn't have much time.

Airgraphs and air letters are practically impossible to get here, so I guess I'll have to just use ordinary mail. It seems to work pretty well, mostly anyway.

* "O.T.U." stands for "Operational Training Unit." Although the majority of Operational Training Units were in Britain, there were a number of them in Canada at which airmen might train before going overseas. George's O.T.U. was at Hixon, Staffordshire.

Doug King bought himself a bicycle yesterday and these bics. over here have the brakes on the handlebars, one for each wheel. Well, Doug used the one on the front wheel and really came a cropper. I guess he went over the handlebars. He has a cut on his head and is limping around. He looks pretty sorry, considering this is his 21st birthday today.

When Dave Harries wrote his letter, he was a bit afraid, I think. Just part of the snow had melted and I think they were practically swimming then. I guess you really had a flood this spring.

Well, I guess this is all I can think of for this time. I was sure pleased to get those letters today.

I hope you are all well.

> Love,
> George.

LETTER 29.

R142247
SGT. KING G.M.
R.C.A.F. OVERSEAS
May 29th, 1943

Dear Mom,

Well, at last I have got some more air letter forms, so I may send home a few quick ones. I got a letter from you today and two yesterday.

I haven't been working so hard these last two or three days, but we were for a couple of weeks. We ended up writing a nav. exam. I came sixth out of 17, so that wasn't bad.

I'm sorry to hear about your back being sore. It always seems to last for a long time and is so miserable. I hope it didn't last long this time. How about Pop—is he okay now? The weather will be pretty nice now, so I hope Dad is okay again.

I got a parcel from Ellen yesterday, a real nice one. I have written to her now. I wrote and thanked Mrs Main twice for the candy. I have written her once a month for the last five months, so I really don't know what is wrong. I have written 57 letters to Canada since the middle of March, so you see no one is not being written to. Mrs Main has had three of them sent to her, and you have had 12—thirteen counting this, and I haven't marked any airgraphs down. You can see from that, Mom, that I am doing my best. I got a letter from Aunt Georgie. She has sent me another carton of cigs. and another parcel. I got her first set, but she hasn't got my letter yet. I have to write one or two letters a night right along. I haven't got Bill's Suns* yet, but I'm looking out for them in the paper box. It will take a little while for them to start coming.

We have got some pictures of the crew, so as soon as we get them back from being developed, I will send them. They are sure a fine bunch of fellows. We should really do good, because there isn't one man who would cause trouble in the crew. It's funny how much you get to think of a bunch like this. It's just like brothers, and we do things for one another like that, too.

You refer[r]ed to my Father and Mother-in-law in your last letter. Well, I'm not just so sure about that. She claims to write an awful lot of letters, but I sure don't get them all.

I got a heck of a bundle from Jim—he must have took an awful fit of writing.

Fisher is coasting along about a month behind me in his training. He still may end up here after a while. I would like to see Buck or Roy

* George's brother Bill was sending him copies of the Grenfell Sun.

again. I get quite a few letters from Fisher.

Well, I guess I am running out of space. I sure hope you are all well at home. I guess you are pretty busy.

Your loving son,
George.

LETTER 30.

R142247
SGT. KING G.M.
R.C.A.F. OVERSEAS
June 4th, 1943

Dear Mom,

Well here I am again. I got a nice big parcel from you two days ago and an air letter today. It was written on May 19, so that was pretty good time. The parcel came over very well, and it just tastes wonderful. How did you ever get so many choc[o]late bars? And gum—it is really nice to have when your[sic] flying. It is a big help to keep your ears from hurting, to say nothing of being a pleasant pass time. The shortbread is really good. You surely must scrimp yourself to make a tin-full like that—it takes a lot of sugar, I know. You really go to too much trouble sending me all the boxes—just too good to me. I was sure glad to see the two "Leaders"* in the box. Say, Mom, the tin of tobacco makes three I have now, so as far as tobacco is concerned, I guess I have enough to last until about '45. I don't mean cigarettes, tho'—I run out of them quite often, but there are 900 on the way, I believe. That is, from you, Jim, and Aunt Georgie.

We are enjoying life pretty well these days. We fly every day, so things never really get dull. This crew I am in are really the nicest

*   George's parents had sent him copies of the Regina Leader-Post.

bunch of chaps I have ever met. I'd say I was really lucky to get in with them. The pictures we took won't be ready for two more weeks, so I guess it will be quite a while until you get them.

It's too bad that Dad's legs get so tired—he will have such a lot to do, and keep his garden as well. You all must be busy all the time.

I think I will sign another two dollars a month home when I get the chance. They have changed the system of pay now, and are not going to keep any deferred pay for us. I should have a bit up in London now, tho'. I think I am allowed to go up and collect it when I have leave, or if I am getting married. I think I'll use the first method to get mine.

Don't mind this—I think it is what's known as doodling.*

We had been having lovely weather here for a while, but it is raining and has been off and on for three days.

This is the writing pad you sent me in the parcel. I sure like this paper.

If the weather would clear up, I think we would get some leave in a few weeks. I'm ready for a bit any time now. I'd like to see the folks at Henley and Aunt Sally, and also nip up to Scotland for a day or two just to look around.

I got a letter from Ken Bourne yesterday, and he is fine. His pilot has got his commission now, so Ken's should be along one of these times. It is getting about time for it for him.

You don't seem to think I am getting your parcels, Mom. I'm afraid it's you not getting my letters. I have got everything you have sent except the last box with the two prs. of shorts and that is just because it hasn't had time to get here yet. I hope you get some of my letters because I write lots of them and it mustn't be nice for you sending all these things and letters with no answers coming to them.

* At this point, George has drawn something unidentifiable on the paper.

Cream sure is a price, isn't it? 41 cents and 44 cents—that is just about a dime higher than it used to be. That seems to make all the work with the cattle worthwhile, doesn't it?

How are the lilac bushes this year? Have they done any blooming for you? I hope they did—they seem so pretty when they bloom.

How long is Mrs Main out at Burnhams' for? I guess G.C.'s* won't care for that, do they?

I guess this is all I have to say for this time, Mom, so I may as well close. I hope you are all well.

> Your loving son,
> George.

LETTER 31.

> Sallie King
> 55 Shirlock Road
> Hampstead N.W.
> London, England
> June 6th, 1943

My dear Agnes & Will,

I was so delighted to get your letter. I began to think you were never going to write, but I see that your letter was dated the 12th of April & I didn't get it until the 31st of May. I was so pleased to know you were all well. I know you must miss the boys. I heard from George that he has been sent on to Stafford so I doubt if I shall see him again for a long time. He may get a long leave next time & be able to get to London.

I expect by this time you are all busy on the farm. I saw Jennie's photo with her husband. George sent it, but I had to return it at once.

* The "G.C.'s" refers to the family of George's uncle, Gordon McCowan.

I do wish she would write to me. Now [that] she is married her time is her own. Give my love to her & tell her how I long to see you all. But that can't be, I suppose.

I am expecting Daisy to come up for the day soon. Kathleen* came up the other day for the day & we had quite a nice time together. She is such a nice girl—you would like her. They are all smitten with George & I think he liked them all, especially Uncle George. Daisy says George doesn't seem very grand again, but I daresay he will pick up now [that] the weather is warmer.

No news now [that] we can't go far out. Everything is quiet & dull for everybody. I hope you & Will are keeping well. Are you rationed like us? But we must not grouse—we are not as bad as some countries. We do get enough to eat of a sort. We could do with more variety—we can't get fresh fruit & what little there is, it's such a price.

I must tell you George did not smoke while he was here. I daresay he had a good go-in when they got outside.

Now I will close. With my fondest love to all. Hoping to hear from you soon. Lottie sends her love.

> Love from your loving Sister,
> Sallie

LETTER 32.

> R142247
> SGT. KING G.M.
> R.C.A.F. OVERSEAS
> June 10th, 1943

Dear Mom,

Here we go again. I've managed to get another of these forms. I

* Kathleen was the daughter of Daisey King, and thus was George's cousin.

* The Scobies, a family from the district, lost a baby, and this is what George refers to here.

† Gordon McCowan's daughter Norma reports that her father often sustained injuries as a result of farming and operating the U.G.G. elevator at Summerberry.

‡ Ralston McFarlane was a relative of Douglas and Robert McFarlane, friends of George's from the Summerberry district.

don't know just what's wrong, Mom, but you don't seem to have got nearly all of my letters. I got the parcels and the shorts a long time ago, and have written you as soon as I got each one. I got a letter from you today telling me of all the accidents in the district. That is surely a shame about Scobies'* baby. He will feel terrible about it, won't he? I guess Gordon's† fingers will be pretty well okay again by now.

I just got one other letter, and it really came as a surprise. It was from Ralston MacFarlane[sic].‡ I could hardly believe my eyes.

We have been doing quite a bit of flying lately. It is getting pretty good. We all know just what one another are like in the air now, and it is easy to fly when you know the other chaps. They are all good men at their jobs, too, as well as being really nice fellows. This little Welshman is just about the cockiest little guy I ever saw—I don't think he would take anything from anyone.

I got two of these blue things today, so I think I'll write Jeannie one, too. I may get more of them from now on as they are getting the post office on this station fairly well organized. I like these best of all—you can get quite a letter on them and they seem fairly fast.

Until today I hadn't heard from anyone for two weeks. It is quite some time since I have heard from Jim. He seems to be kept pretty busy with his work down east, doesn't he? Does he know when he is going to take his leave yet? If I was him, I think I'd take it around the end of June and the first of July. I may get some leave sometime soon, so I may see Uncle George and Aunt Sally again soon. I haven't heard from Uncle George lately, but he doesn't write often anyway.

I guess this is all for this time. Give my love to Dad and Bill.

Your loving son,
George.

LETTER 33.

R142247
SGT. KING G.M.
R.C.A.F. OVERSEAS
June 25th, 1943

Dear Mom,

Well here I am again, a bit late this time as I have just finished a few days' leave. I spent it with Uncle George. We really had a nice time together. They are all fine at Henley.

I got a letter from you this morning and was glad to hear you are all well. It will be nice if Les* gets the school at Fleming. That is more or less Verda's home town, isn't it?

Tell Dad that Henley is really beautiful now, just a picture.† There was sure a crowd there on Sunday boating, and soon I also met one of Dad's old chums. I've heard Dad speak of him a lot—Cory Lawrence.

All your parcels are getting here. Sometimes they take a couple of months, but they do get here. I got Aunt May's parcel too.

I don't doubt Pat may not want to talk to you, but if her mother cares to be silly…‡

I'll write an ordinary letter in a day or two. I have quite a few to write. I guess this is all I have room for this time.

Your loving son,
George.

* George's uncle Les McCowan was a teacher, and his wife's name was Verda.

† Henley-on-Thames was William King's home town, but he never visited it again after he left England for Canada at age 17 in 1890.

‡ Patsy was the daughter of the United Church minister, and this may have caused a rift of some sort between her mother and Agnes, who was a devout member of the United Church. From all accounts, George and Patsy were a rather wild pair, and this may have been the source of some friction.

LETTER 34.

R142247
SGT. KING G.M.
R.C.A.F. OVERSEAS
June 26th, 1943

Dear Dad,

This should be a pretty long letter, as I have just finished a visit with Uncle George at your old home town. It is sure lovely now.

Uncle George is fine—he carries his age very well. It is a really nice little house he has—at least he has part of it. Two fair-sized rooms, one for a living room and the other a bedroom. Then there is a little sort of back kitchen he keeps a lot of stuff in. Of course, there is the usual very small room at the back.* Taking it all around, it is just right for him. He works for the Old Folks' Home every other week, but he says he spends most of his time waiting for them to get leather.† He seems to have a fair amount of money, and manages very well. We sure had a good time together.

When I got there, my shoes were in pretty poor shape at the heels, and you can't get them repaired here, so as soon as he saw them, he got to work and in no time at all he had me a new pair of heels put on. Uncle is sure good at it, just like you. The shoes are splitting at the sides, so I guess I'll have to get you to take some money out of one of my cheques and send me a pair over. You can't buy them without coupons here, and we aren't given any, so I'm just out of luck.

We went down and looked over the regatta course and all that. The hills on the far side of the river are really beautiful now. There was sure a crowd there on Sunday afternoon—hundreds of people were rowing. We watched them let some boats through the lock.

* George is referring euphemistically to the lavatory.

† Both William King and his brother George had trained as cobblers. For this reason, when William served in the Boer War, he was made an infantryman so that he could repair boots.

There are still lots of swans on the river there, too. I always remember you telling us about the swans there.

When we were having our little stroll down by the river on Sunday night, we met Cory Lawrence. I have heard you speak of him a lot, and was really pleased when I heard who it was. So was he. He looked me over from head to foot and then said there was a big resemblance between us, or as he said, "You can see old Bill there alright." Just what do they mean, Dad, when they start talking about you and say, "He was a boy"? I'm afraid you must have been quite a b———r in your time over here.

Aunt Dais is really good to me. I always go over to her place to sleep. Tom still is very much a Canadian. In fact, he prefers it to England quite a bit, and likes to talk about Canada always.

We are doing some night flying just now. It is about 11.50 and we are waiting to go up. We don't go till 1.30. I'm afraid I'll be pretty sleepy by the time we get down, but there is all tomorrow to sleep, so I guess I'll pull through, though.

We will be through here after a while—about four weeks—and I should be able to get some leave and go to Uncle George's again and see Aunt Sally too. Some leave I will go up to Scotland. I'd like to see some of Scotland, too, but all the leave I've got so far are[sic] not enough to see Uncle George and go anywhere else on it too between times seeing them. It is as close to getting home as I can get. Uncle George is so much like you, especially his voice and what he says.

I think I'll enclose a snap of my pilot and bomb aimer and I. You will be able to tell which is Norm Spencer by the wing he is wearing, and of course you know me, so Doug Wylie is the other one.

Well, Dad, I guess this is about all for this time. Don't you work too hard in that garden of yours. I know you like it, and it is always a

Doug Wylie, Norm Spencer, and George at O.T.U., summer 1943.

real credit to you, but with all the other work you have to do, there is no sense in you hurting yourself.

Give my love to Mom and Bill.

Your loving son,
George.

LETTER 35.

R142247
SGT. KING G.M.
R.C.A.F. OVERSEAS
June 30th, 1943

Dear Jean,

I intended to get this letter away to you before this, but I have been rather busy for the last few days. What I want you to do for me if you will is to get Mom a nice present for her birthday for me. I'll write and tell them to send you the money and you can tell them how much it is. You see, I can't send money over. I just have to have it taken out of what I have signed over. You know what to get better than I do. Either something for her house or to wear—just what you think best. I was thinking of something around twenty bucks.* I guess I told you in my last letter I had had a few days' leave and went to see Uncle George. He is fine. I'm doing some night flying right now. It won't be long until I have some more leave. Wish I could get to Wilkie on it, but that day should come. I guess I'm out of room just now.

Your loving brother,
George.

* $20 in 1943 would be about $225 in today's currency.

LETTER 36.

R142247
SGT. KING G.M.
R.C.A.F. OVERSEAS
July 2nd, 1943

Dear Mom,

I guess it is just about time for me to drop you a line. This letter won't get to you for your birthday.* I have tried to arrange something with Jeannie for your birthday. It is really hard when you can't send things or money from here. Jeannie will send to you for the money after she gets the present for me. It isn't a very good way, but it is really the best I can manage.

We had a day off yesterday, so we went to a little town about 17 miles from here and met the nicest old lady—she had a little sort of boarding house. It was her birthday today and [she] was 68. She ended up kissing us all goodbye. Her son had been to Canada to train in the Air Force and people treated him very well over there so she was doing her best to return the favor, and did a very good job of it.

It looks as though I have to go for this time, Mom, but I will finish off later.

Well, I had to quit for a while as I have been very busy doing cross-countries and had to do a lot of flight planning. That took up my afternoon and we flew at night. Then, the next morning I had to sleep. But it looks like a little break just now, so I guess I had better finish the letter while I can.

We should have leave in about 2 wks again, I think, so I guess I'll go and see Aunt Sally as well as Uncle George. Aunt Dais and Aunt Sally have made up a plan where I go to Henley for the first part of

* Agnes King's birthday was 17 July.

Left, George at O.T.U., summer 1943.

84

Above, comrades-in-arms, O.T.U., summer 1943. Left to right, Bill Baker, Harold Hicks, Doug Wylie, Norm Spencer, and George.

† George is referring to "Sweet Caporal" cigarettes.

my leave and take Aunt Dais to London and would visit with Aunt Sally, so I should have lots to tell you after that's over.

There sure isn't much happening around here these days. There are some W.A.A.F.* dances here, but I never care much for dances on the station anyway.

I like the view Dad takes of Pat and I not agreeing anymore [and] not having to go to church anymore. A fine thing, letting me spoil your religion.

I'm afraid I'll have to quit pretty soon with this letter and write some more. I'm really way behind. Gladys Taylor wrote me quite a good letter, like she always writes—witty as ever.

Look, Mom, I am enclosing some pictures this time. I'll just write their names on the back. There was one of me taken, but it's ghastly. Norm took it just as I turned around, and it blurred.

Well, Mom, I guess I'll close for now.

Your loving son,
George.

LETTER 37.

R142247
SGT. KING G.M.
R.C.A.F. OVERSEAS
July 12th, 1943

Dear Mom,

Well, here goes again. I received a carton of sweet Caps.† from you today, and was very pleased to get them as I was right out of Canadian cigarettes. Thanks very much—it was sure good of you to send them.

I'm doing a lot of thinking about you lately, Mom, more than usual as your birthday is only 5 days away and I still haven't managed to get a telegram away. I haven't been able to get to town for five days now because we are getting our flights cancelled because of bad weather and can't get our time in as we can't get out. I really feel quite bad about it. I hope Jeannie gets her instructions soon enough so you will get your present fairly close to the right time.

I hope you and Dad got up to Pinkham and Wilkie* okay. I guess you would really have a nice time. I sure hope you did have.

That would be something for Bill to have Norma and Jean cooking for him. I'll bet they are good, too.

We are going to be all through here in a little over a week, so I guess I will be able to see Aunt Sally. I sent her some things I got in parcels. Aunt Annie sent me some tea and sugar for Aunt Sally, so I sent that and a lot of other stuff too. Pudding powders, soup, etc. It is sure nice to go and see Uncle George—he is so much like Dad it is nearly like home.

I really haven't much time, Mom, so I guess I had better close for this time. I have a lot to do. I will write again tomorrow or the next day.

Your loving son,
George.

* Agnes' daughter Jeanne lived at Wilkie, Saskatchewan, and her sister Annie lived at Pinkham, Saskatchewan.

Graduation from O.T.U. at Hixon, Staffordshire, July 1943. Front row: second from left, George King; third from left, Bill Baker; sixth from left, Doug Wylie; seventh from left, Norm Spencer; eighth from left, Harold Hicks.

LETTER 38.

C.N. Telegraphs
R142247
SGT. KING G.M.
R.C.A.F. OVERSEAS
July 17th, 1943

Mrs. Wm. King, Summerberry Sask.,

Loving birthday greetings. You are more than ever in my thoughts at this time.

George King.

LETTER 39.

C.P. Telegraphs
R155809
LAC KING J.
R.C.A.F. OVERSEAS.
NFLD.
July 17th, 1943

Mrs. W. King, Summerberry,

For every birthday and every day between I wish you the best of everything.

Jim King.

LETTER 40.

R142247
SGT. KING G.M.
R.C.A.F. OVERSEAS
July 20th, 1943

Dear Mom,

Here I am again. I have just received the parcel with the shirts, socks, handkerchiefs, and tea, and was very pleased to get them. The shirts are slightly large, but I'm sure they will shrink to just the right size. I also got parcels from Jeannie and Auntie Annie. I can start up a drug store any time now—I have enough shaving cream to last me for life, if I live to be 100. My friend Taffy* can use some of it, anyway, so it is okay. The Homemakers sent me 300 cigarettes the other day, so it seems I'm sure not forgotten. Tell Dad that he has at least two letters coming from me now and there will [be] another any day now. I don't know what to do about my girlfriend—she has started writing again. I really don't know what to do. Our crew are doing very well here. They are the nicest bunch of guys I ever met. I'd never want to fly with anyone else.

Your loving son,
George.

*   "Taffy" was the nickname of Harold Hicks, the Wireless Operator.

88

Aug 21/43.

Dear Jim:

Well you long-legged old bug[?]
I guess its time I was tossing
another bundle at you.
I received 300 sweet caps for
you yesterday, which was quite
a welcome sight and reminds
me I had better light up
right about now, I'm lit up
just with a cigarette tho'. I have
quite a cold and am crappy in
just now.

I am at a hell of a nice
station now a real good mess. Just
three of us in our room. Bill Baker
Bill Morement and I. It is one of those
stations where the shit flies at
times, you know what I mean.
Will I've told Mom I'm still
training; so if anything should

LETTER 41.

R142247
SGT. KING G.M.
R.C.A.F. OVERSEAS
July 24th, 1943

Dear Dad,

Well, Pop, I guess you will be thinking it is time I was writing. I have just had some leave and changed stations* and given Henley another going over.

Uncle George is fine, and we had our usual good time together.† Aunt Dais and Tom are fine. Phil and his wife came down this time. Phil and Tom are a lot alike—I like them both. I still didn't have enough time to go and see Aunt Sally too, but I'm not so far away from her now. I think I will be able to see her if I get a 48 or 36. I sent Aunt Sally a collection of stuff I got out of parcels just before I went on leave—some tea and sugar Aunt Annie sent to me for her, and some other things I just sent her out of my parcels. She sent a letter right back and seemed quite pleased with the things.

I met an old pal of yours again this time, Dad. He is Tom Godley. You and him had a set of boxing gloves between you. He seemed quite pleased to see me, and was interested to know how you were.

I hope Mom got her cable not too long after her birthday. I know it would be late, but that was my first chance to send one. I hope you had a nice time at Wilkie and Pinkham. I guess Bill would have quite a time with his two housekeepers. I guess they will be pretty good at it, too.

I met young Les in London on my way back to this place from Henley. He is pretty well fed up with the whole thing. He says it seems

* By this time, George was stationed at a Conversion Unit in Waterbeach, Cambridgeshire, where he was training in Stirling heavy bombers.

† George provides Jim with a more candid description of this "good time" in letter 42.

90

† Had he received his commission, George would have been a Flying Officer.

as though he will never get anything to do, but he looks well, anyway.

Henley still gets lots of crowds there. I went down there on a Sunday morning, and there were really crowds going in from London for the day. Between Slough, Maidenhead, and Henley, they emptied the train.

We have a mid-upper gunner and a flight engineer now.* That makes seven in the crew—five Canadians and Taffy Hicks our little Welshman, and now a man from Lancashire. Bill Moreman[sic] is his name. He seems like quite a nice chap, but I've only met him so far. Taffy is a day late getting back now and he still isn't here, so I guess he is in trouble by now.

I was recommended for a commission from O.T.U.† I don't suppose it means much, but it makes me feel good anyway—just a few of the navigators were recommended.

The wheat should be coming along pretty fair by now. I guess you will be starting to cut about a month from now. How was the hay situation this year? And how are the crops anyway? Ellen said things were getting very dry out there. That is sure a change from last year, but good old Sask. is always full of surprises. I hope it isn't too dry.

I haven't heard from Jim for some time now. I guess he will be getting home on leave soon.

We are flying in great big kites now—they are Stirlings. I don't know whether you have heard of them or not.

Well, Dad, I guess this is all for this time. I hope I hear from you again soon.

Your loving son,
George.

LETTER 42.

R142247
SGT. KING G.M.
R.C.A.F. OVERSEAS
July 25th, 1943

Dear Jim,

Well you old son-of-a-(guess what?), how are you? How long is it since you've heard from me and all that? I've just finished a seven day leave and worked like a pisser before that, so I'm behind in my letter writing. I came to this new station the night before last, and fuck a sad duck if I didn't meet Hank Hea* here at dinner time. He has just been here for a couple of weeks, so we will be together for two weeks at least, and seeing we are on the same kind of kites may go to the same squadron together. The kites, by the way, are Stirlings.

I was down to Uncle George's and Phil was down at the same time. By God, Phil, Tom, and Uncle George all pack a lot of liquor—it was all I could do to keep up to them. By God, we really had a few binges, and then I had some more in London with the boys and ended up meeting Les McCowan there. He seems pretty well browned with the whole thing.

I hope you can read this letter, but my pen has gone for a shit on me and this is all I have to write with tonite.†

I probably told you we have a Canadian mid-upper, a P/O from Toronto, and now we have our Engineer, a boy from Lancashire. He seems okay—I don't know him very well yet.

I just bummed another chap's pen, so you will be able to read a bit of this, anyway.

Bill Baker and I campaigned London together for a couple of days

*   "Hank Hea" refers to Riley Hea of Summerberry.

†   The first part of this letter is written in pencil.

92

and had a piss of a time. We went to two shows. 12 shillings and 9'6 seeing your[sic] a bloody Canadian—about $3.00 and $2.40.

The last nite we were there a pilot by the name of Russell—a hell of a good guy—and I took a couple of women home and couldn't get a bus or train back, so we walked in London in the blackout for about 7 miles. I was nearly sober by the time I got back.

By God, when I get back here I find there still is a lot for me to learn.

Say, I'm in and out of the shit so many times with Patsy that I hardly know where I stand. She has taken to sending me letters just lately—air letters—and wants to know just what is it that makes me such an unfaithful wretch, so if you happen to have your leave in September, just tell her that I'm not that sort of a shit at all. She is having her holidays in Sept. Oh, yes, if you can get in there yourself, well a King has done it before, but I hope you can do the job better.

While I'm on the subject, how about Pt. Hawkesbury and St John's? Who's winning?*

Well, I seem to be running out of news, so I guess I'll quit and write another letter. I'm really behind.

> Your loving brother,
> George.

* George is asking Jim here which of two girlfriends he currently has "on the go"—one from Port Hawkesbury or one from St John's.

LETTER 43.

R142247
SGT. KING G.M.
R.C.A.F. OVERSEAS
July 28th, 1943

Dear Mom,

Just received a swell big parcel from you today sent on June 15. I haven't got a letter from you for a while, but seeing I've had leave and moved from the last station, there will be some letters to catch up to me yet.

This new station isn't bad at all. We have nice big aircraft and a picture show on the station six nites a week. We aren't so far from London here, so I may get in to see Aunt Sally some time. I don't know whether Dad has my letter or not, but I've told him all about my leave at Henley. I sure had a nice time there. They are all so nice to me.

Say, Mom, I have most of one tin of pipe tobacco and have two more full ones. I am sending one of those to Phil, so I guess you needn't send me any more for quite a while.

Well, I am trying a new system of sending mail. Tell me how it gets there with this system, because there is lots of room for writing in this way.

There are seven men in the crew now—a mid-upper gunner, Ray Eberly[sic], and an Engineer, Bill Moreman[sic]. Ray is a Canadian, and Bill is from Lancashire. They are a nice pair of chaps, too. Of course, there are still the original five of us.

I really got a surprise the second day I came here. I was sitting in the mess reading the paper, and someone came up and said, "Is that you, George?" and there was Riley Hea. He just got here a couple of weeks before I did, so we will be together for a few weeks. It is sure nice to see him again, but we haven't had much time together yet because he is working at nite and I'm working in the day, but we have had two or three good long talks about old times. It's sure great to be able to do that—it seems quite a while ago now.

I guess you and Dad had quite a nice little holiday this summer—you deserve it. I hope you had a nice time. Jean and Bruce have a nice little place, haven't they?

There is no barber on this station, and Bill Baker and I are going around like a couple of musicians. We can't get one for some time, either, so I think I'll buy a fiddle.

I did very well at O.T.U.—just about the best in the course—and got recommended for a commission, but it appears that that doesn't go for anything now [that] I have changed commands, but it should help when the time comes.

I really tried hard to get that cable to you, but the best I could do was get it away on your birthday, so it would be a bit late. I just couldn't get into town to send it until my leave came.

Aunt Lizzie* has been writing me quite a few letters lately. She didn't seem to mind me getting her home town mixed up with Edinburough[sic]. In fact, she didn't mention it in her letter. Ellen wrote me one too. Pat is really what I can't figure out. She is sending heaps of letters again, but I imagine I'll be in the doghouse pretty well permanently as I have written one in six weeks.

When is Jim getting home for his leave? I guess it will be pretty nice for him. We sure had a good time last year.

How are Dad and Bill these days? I guess everyone is pretty busy now. I hope Dad is not working too hard. Well, goodbye for this time.

> Your loving son,
> George.

* George's Aunt Lizzie was married to Agnes' brother, David McCowan.

LETTER 44.

R142247
SGT. KING G.M.
R.C.A.F. OVERSEAS
August 2nd, 1943

Dear Mom,

I just wrote a few days ago—that was an air mail letter—but I got one from you just two days ago, so I guess it's time I wrote again.

Uncle Ernest* sent me a carton of 300 cigs that I got today, so I have written Aunt Annie and him a letter tonite.

You wanted to know about my money. Well, the govt. were holding some back as deferred pay, but they stopped that a month ago and we get it all now, so I was going to sign over $10 a month more. Now we have found out that we have been F/Sgts. since the 23rd of April, so I was waiting for that to come and sign $15 more instead of $10, but there seems to be a lot of red tape and if it doesn't come through in the next two wks., I am signing the ten over anyway. I know what I save seems to be a poor effort, but this country is really hard on money right now. You have to pay 4 shillings for a decent meal in the town where we are. So you can see a dollar for a meal, that it isn't cheap. I hope I have accounted for myself on that score now.

And now, Mom, you told me a long time ago that it took two to cause any trouble. Well, there sure was two in any trouble Pat and I had because there has never been a time when I haven't had more letters sent to me than I had written, so I guess she got sick of it for a while, but I have had a lot of letters lately. I do appreciate your getting so annoyed and indignant about the whole thing, Mom, but I can really take care of myself very well, and no one ever gets anything

*   Ernest Taylor, who married Annie McCowan, was George's uncle, and operated a store in Pinkham, Saskatchewan.

much over me.

It's sure great to see Riley Hea around, but he is leaving in about 5 days, but it has sure been swell to get together again. Riley is just the same as ever.

I guess you will be pretty busy these days. I hope you and Dad are not working too hard. How is Bill these days? Give my love to them both.

> Your loving son,
> George.

LETTER 45.

R142247
SGT. KING G.M.
R.C.A.F. OVERSEAS
August 4th, 1943

Dear Jim,

Hello cock, and how are you? I'm up the … I mean in the pink. I wrote you an air letter last week, so I'll send you a long slow one this time. There is bugger all interesting to tell you, but I'll try to make up something.

Bill Baker has gone on a week's special course in gunnery, so things are a little dull for me just now, but seeing I met Riley Hea on this station I had one wild nite this week. Hank ended the nite collapsing in his bed dead to the world, but I survived to get back to my own barracks. We sure gave old times a going-over that nite. Riley is leaving tomorrow, so I guess I will have to uphold S'berry by myself again. The trouble is, no one is on this station any length of time, so that is the natural place for me to meet some old friends.

I guess the little babe in London will have given me up. I neglected to answer her registered letter, so I guess she hasn't much choice.

I really didn't think anything of these aircraft when I first came here, but now [that] I have flown in them and read the figures, they strike me as being the kind of thing that just isn't the bloody craze, but is just as bloody good or a little better.

There are less Canadians on this station than any other station I've ever been on in my life, but it's okay. The food isn't as good as some, but it's fair, and I'm not losing a bloody pound.

I got a bloody hair cut today, the first one for a bloody month. By Jesus I needed it. Bill Baker was a damn sight worse when he left here. Maybe he has got one since then, though. He is absolutely the wittiest bugger I ever met, only he does mix a good deal of filth in with his wit.

Dick Boulter and I are separated now. We had been together since A.O.S. in Regina. We are a hell of a long way apart now.

I was up at 6 o'clock this morning to fly. That is the earliest I have been up since Brandon Manning. My God it was an effort.

I got quite a nice letter from Noreen Fleming the other day, with the most catty thing I have ever seen in my life in it. She said she had seen Pat about a month before she wrote, but she wouldn't tell me just what she looked like because it was early in the morning. I thought that was very nice of her. Pat doesn't say much for herself these days, but you should see Mrs King get in there and try and break everything all to shit. Nothing is worrying me, but I am getting a hell of a kick out of it.

When are you taking your leave this year? You have my full permission to throw a scud at the parsonette* if you get a chance, and

* George refers to Patsy as the "Parsonette," since she was the United Church minister's daughter.

98

have my blessings. In fact, take a double header if you can, one for me, as I was never man enough to do it myself.

I guess it is tea time, so I will scuttle off and have it, and finish this later.

5/8/43. So I had tea, then a Scotch and a couple of pints, and then to the picture show on the station. So that leaves me a fine cunt and the letter isn't finished. The show was "Dr Gillespie's New Assistants," and wasn't bad. I saw "The Pride of the Yankees" a few days ago and it was just as good as the first time I saw it, but baseball and my mind were always my two weak points, anyway.

There were these Land Army girls at the show. They must have come from a farm near here somewhere, so I think I'll have to walk around to some of the farms one of these days as two of them were okay, by God.

Normie Spencer got a couple of parcels today, so I guess we eat again.

We were up at 6:15 to fly this morning, but it is one o'clock and we are still on the dick—bad weather.

This bloody Bomb Aimer of ours, Doug Wylie, still holds the world's record for being a wolf, but he is one of these gentlemanly wolves. Everything strictly above board, but he sure turns into a stud when he sees a skirt.

We are in the middle of a plum orchard here, so we have a nice time some nites. Red Smalley and I got some dandies last nite. The good way to get them is to go directly passed[sic] the "Out of Bounds" notice and all the best ones are right there. I guess that is because some people believe in signs.

Well, I guess I get paid tomorrow. That will sure as hell be a change. We haven't been paid since July 15, so that makes about 20 days since I've had any pay, and 7 days' leave since then.

Well, Jim, I guess this is about all I can say for this time, so I'll close. Hoping to hear from you soon.

> Your loving bro.,
> George.

P.S. Lay off the canine. G.K.

LETTER 46.

R142247
SGT. KING G.M.
R.C.A.F. OVERSEAS
August 9th, 1943

Dear Mom,

Just a few lines to let you know that I got your air mail letter written on July 18. I was pleased to get it and hear that you had got your present. I'm sure pleased at what your[sic] getting—it was just something like that I had in mind.

It was nice you had a nice time on your little trip. I'll bet the clan had a great old get-together. The King clan had a little get-together over here just about the same time, with Phil, Tom, and the two Georges. These Kings over here are sure a great bunch—no fuss or anything. I was just one of them. It was sure nice.

I am having a bit of a dull time just now, as we are working all day and part of the nite. I haven't been out for eight days now, so I am having a good chance to recover financially from my leave. Speaking of leave, I guess Jim should have had his by now. It's too bad he didn't get it around the end of June or the first of July—there is always more doing around home then than any other time.

My God, that was an awful fine Bill Harries had to pay. That will take the cows a week to pay for it. It won't just be the nite of the party Bill milks them for nothing. That was funny about Jimmie Harries being taken as an "A" man.*

Aunt Lizzie writes me quite a few letters, always very nice ones, and has sent me socks, parcels, and cigarettes. Uncle Ernest has sent me cigarettes, too. Seeing Bill Baker's parcels aren't arriving yet, the cigarettes don't last so long with both of us smoking them.

I thought these guys at Cambridge University just wore their gowns on special occasions, but doggonit they wear them all the time.

We are going to fly tonite, but I still have about an hour to wait.

We'll be leaving here in a couple of weeks, but I don't think we will be moving very far from here.

I think I prefer the Midlands, but this part is okay. There is a lot of flat country around here, and lots of wheat, but it is all cut and stacked now.

I guess this is all I have room for. Give my love to Dad and Bill.

Your loving son,
George.

LETTER 47.

R142247
SGT. KING G.M.
R.C.A.F. OVERSEAS
August 20th, 1943

Dear Mom, Dad & Bill,

Here I am again, a little bit later than usual, but I have been doing some more moving, and I'm with Riley Hea† again. I just met him this morning, so it seems like old times again.

I received a real nice parcel from you just before I left the last station, Mom—gum, choc[o]late bars, and handkerchiefs. It came over fine, and I was glad to get it. You are really too good to me.

I got letters from Aunt Georgie, Aunt May, and cigarettes from Jim and Dave Harries. That is sure good of Davey, isn't it? You wouldn't see many boys that would do that just for a friend.

The weather here is very hot just now. My hands are so sticky I can hardly write.

This is just about the nicest station I've ever been at. The food is first class, and there are just three of us in our room—Bill Baker the rear gunner, and Bill Morement our Engineer. So we have things just as we want them, and it's one of these stations where everyone is friendly. There can sure be a difference in the personnel, and this is the best. I'm really pleased with it.

Things will really be happening at home now, I guess. Harvest should be in full swing. I guess you will be busy. Jim should be home in a very few days now.*

Poor Bill won't have time to turn around these days. Oh well, Bill, keep up the good work. You'll have help next year—that's a promise.

I was really gallant the other nite. Doug Wylie—that's our Air Bomber—and I were walking home and met a W.A.A.F. we know with her bicycle, so Doug took the W.A.A.F. and I took her bic. It was a long time since I've had a good bic. ride, so I enjoyed myself quite well.†

I'm sure doing lots of training. I don't know when I'll be finished being U.T. air crew.‡

Have you still got a ban on the ministry, Mom?§ What was that news you were talking about? Was it just what I wrote in my letter, or did you have some fresh stuff in the home town?

I got a letter from Uncle George the other day. They are all fine

* George's brother Jim was coming home on leave from Scoudouc, New Brunswick.

† In letter 48, George provides Jim with a more colourful version of this story.

‡ John Zinkhan, a former RCAF navigator, says that "U.T." was not a formal RCAF acronym of which he is aware.

§ Agnes' "ban on the ministry" had something to do with the feud with Patsy and her parents. Patsy's father was the United Church minister at Summerberry.

* Andy Emke owned a store in Summerberry, and that would explain why his business was ruined by rationing.

† Bill Harries farmed near Summerberry on Rod Christie's land.

‡ Miss Cumming was a former teacher of Agnes' who lived in Liverpool, where Agnes lived for a time with her family before they moved to Australia, then to New Zealand, and finally to Canada.

§ George was initially stationed at Bournemouth on the south coast of England.

** "Dinty" Moore was a bachelor farmer from the Summerberry district, but the meaning of this reference to him is unclear.

down at Henley. I guess I'll be back there in another couple of months or so.

We have a great supply of records for our little gramophone now. Every time anyone goes to town they bring about four back with them. Normie and I got six the other day.

I'm glad the shoes are on the way. My old Oxfords are pretty gruesome just now.

Who is going to do your threshing this year, or do you know yet? Is old Andy Emke* still in the business? That is—threshing? I guess all the rationing has ruined his other business for the duration.

Bill Harries must have really been having himself a great time the night the cop put the stop to his fun. That's just like poor old Bill to get himself into a jam. How are Gladys and Wallace making out at Rod's?†

How is Mrs. Eagle? Is she still living in Grenfell? If I knew where she was, I could write to her. The poor soul must be very lonesome—which she is.

I don't believe I will ever be able to look Miss Cumming‡ up, Mom. I don't think that I would want to take up any of my leave to do it, and that is right out of my part of the country. I have a definite part of the country for the rest of my stay over here now, and it isn't that part.

I got a letter from Reg Barber. He is where I put in my first three months in the country, quite a lovely spot. I believe you know where that was.§

Doug King has gone a long way from here now, a very long way, but I won't be moving like that. It would be interesting just the same.

I got one of the "Suns" the other day. That is the first one, and it sure looked good. The new editor doesn't seem to have Dinty's** fire, but he does okay. There were three "Leaders" in the last parcel—that really pleased me. Now I'm waiting for this one with the shoes to see what Bob Scofield has been up to. Maybe it's another of his line-shoots.* Bob was good at that.

I've just been over for supper, and is it ever a change from the last station, really a treat.

Well, folks, I guess this is all for this time. I hope you are all well and not working hard. I'm really pleased at what you are getting with the birthday money, Mom. I sure hope you like what you get.

> Lots of love to all,
> George.

LETTER 48.

R142247
SGT. KING G.M.
R.C.A.F. OVERSEAS
August 21st, 1943

Dear Jim,

Well, you long-legged old bugger, I guess it's time I was tossing another bundle at you.

I received 300 sweet Caps. from you yesterday, which was quite a welcome sight, and reminds me—I had better light up right about now. I'm lit up—just with a cigarette, tho'! I have quite a cold, and am staying in just now.

I am at one hell of a nice station now—a real good mess. Just three of us in our room—Bill Baker, Bill Morement and I. It is one of those stations where the shit flies at times—you know what I mean.

Well, I've told Mom I'm still training, so if anything should happen—not that it is at all likely to—you could just enlighten her that I wasn't training when it did.

We have had a couple of good nites in the pubs lately. Bill Baker

* Bob Scofield was a serviceman from Summerberry district. A "line-shoot" was slang for an exaggerated story – "bullshit," in today's terminology.

and I sounded up on a lot of those good old songs that you never sing at church one night. I guess it was really a racket—very amusing, to say the least.

I guess poor old Noreen has taken the horse good and proper this time. That is sure as hell a change for her. She always got her own way pretty well. She told me she was all through with Fat in a letter quite a long time ago, but I didn't write and ask if she was available or not. Maybe it would be worth looking into. You, old bugger, are going on leave Monday, I believe. This letter should welcome you back to Scoudouc, so maybe you will have looked the situation over. You never were a man to pass up an opportunity, and she always did have a comfortable look about her. I wouldn't mind "having a do" myself.

You will see from my expression I am getting to be quite a limey. But it is funny how many English expressions a person does pick up after a time. I thought Ken Bourne was funny at Xmas time, but I've been over a hell of a lot longer now than he was then, so I guess I'm a real damn queer by now.

I guess Mom will give you an enraged account of "Me and My Gal." She doesn't know a bloody quarter of the story, and every so often I would make some crack in my letters. She has got it boiled down that Patsy has given me the old go-by, and is in a righteous rage and devotes about a page [in] every letter [to] giving her shit. God Damn, but it is funny after the shit I have been [in] with Patsy. I don't think Mom ever did like her—with the aid of Mrs G.C.,* of course.

By God, Jim! There is the prettiest W.A.A.F. I've ever seen in my life working in our mess. I haven't got around to talking to her yet, but I'm sure going to manage it some way. There really are a nice collection of W.A.A.F.'s here, but this one is the best I've ever seen. She is the kind that makes strong men weak and weak men weaker. So I'm weaker every time I take a look at her. But don't get any notions

* "Mrs G.C." refers to Ellen McCowan, George's aunt.

about my weakness. I could still flatten hell out of you, you great, long, lanky, high-assed old shit. "Take that, by God!"

So far this is a good hot letter, so I am going to send it air mail so it won't lose any of its sting by the time it gets to you.

The last letter I got from Buck Fisher—that was only a week ago—he was doing fine. He still shoots the same old shit.

I haven't been doing much about the fairer sex lately. Doug Wylie and I were rolling home pretty well stewed one nite and met a W.A.A.F. with her bicycle, so that was one too many, and I was tired, so I volunteered to take the bic. and Doug took the W.A.A.F. It was a little woman's bicycle, so I did some wild bloody riding. I don't know what kind of condition it was in the next day, but it sure took one hell of a beating that nite. Doug Wylie said he thought it was the fastest he had ever seen a bic. being ridden. I ended up returning the bicycle and kissing the W.A.A.F. good nite, too, so I think I did pretty fair for me.

Ken Bourne is back on ops. again in a different kind of kite. I guess he will never be as happy again now [that] he has lost his Boston.* That was a pretty tough break. For my part, a Stirling is the best there is. Riley Hea will tell you the same. Of course, Hank and I are on the same station. Hank is the same old guy—quite a boy to say the least.

I got a letter from Scub the other day—what a bloody man. The same old Scub. He writes just like he talks. It's pretty amusing in print—you can imagine that.

I guess Red Fleming will be here pretty soon if he isn't by now. I'll have to sound up on these guys and give them all the shit seeing I'm a vet. in the outfit.

Well, you old ( ). I won't say it—it isn't polite. I hope you had a bloody good leave and entertained the Wolseley locals in the fine

* Ken Bourne's "Boston" was a Douglas Boston light bomber. It may have been destroyed, or withdrawn from service, meaning that he had to fly operations in a different aircraft. Although George was not yet aware of it, by the time he wrote this letter, Ken Bourne had been killed in action.

fashion we did last year, and I hope to have a full account of it from you soon.

> Your loving bro.,
> George.

P.S. Keep it cocked. G.K.

LETTER 49.

R142247
SGT. KING G.M.
R.C.A.F. OVERSEAS
August 28th, 1943

Dear Mom,

Here goes again. I received a letter from you yesterday written on Aug. 10, so it came over pretty well. I was glad to hear everyone was well. I guess Jim will be home just now—you will really have a good time when he is there.

I am a bit behind in my letters just now. It is a week since I have written to you. I mostly manage one every four or five days. The mail isn't getting here quite as good as usual just now, but it seems as though one comes from you just about every week, whether the rest get here or not. You always use these blue ones—they seem to be the most reliable of all. I haven't heard the results of my 1'3* letters to you yet, but Normie found they got to his wife very well.

I hope you have got the pictures I sent you of the boys. Jeannie has got two and thought they were okay.

I think we may be going to a dance in the village tonight. I don't do much dancing these days, as my shoes are in pretty bad shape, and you can picture me trying to dance in these big ones of ours. But I

*   A "1'3 letter" was a more expensive form of air mail, costing one shilling threepence.

guess I will be off to a fresh start when the ones you sent me get here.

So my Father has started falling down the steps of grocery stores? And he told me in a letter that Black always had the "sold out" sign up. Tsk Tsk.

Jean wrote me a letter a little while ago with a picture of Barbara and Norma and her. It is sure a swell snap. The girls sure look nice. Norma seems to have turned into a real lady, and Barbara is really cute. Jeannie seems her over-swelt self as usual.

We are in a nice barracks now. Just three of us in the room. Bill Baker and I piled in the room together, of course, and Billie Morement, our engineer, is in with us. He is a nice little chap. I guess I told you he comes from Lancashire.

The harvest should be pretty well on now, as you had done a couple of days' cutting in the last letter I got. I hope you are all well.

> Your loving son,
> George.

LETTER 50.*

> R142247
> SGT. KING G.M.
> R.C.A.F. OVERSEAS
> September 17th, 1943

Dear Mom,

This is really late this time. I have just had a few days' leave and was to Doug Wylie's brother's wedding in London.† It was quite an event and seeing he is over here and his home is in Toronto he got us to come there as support for his side. Doug was the best man and Bill and Normie and I graced the front seat on the right hand side. Bill Baker and I went to Edinburgh for a day before the wedding and went

* This letter was written 5 days before George was killed. Agnes has written on the envelope, "The Last Letter," since other than a small airgraph, it was the last one that he wrote her and mailed himself. She received it on October 12th, three weeks after he was killed. In late November 1943, she received a final letter that George had written but not mailed before he was killed (see letter 79).

† Newton Wylie, brother of Bomb Aimer Doug Wylie, was married in London on 11 September 1943. There is an account of this in the excerpt from Doug Wylie's diary, on page 151.

* George and his crew had bombed Berlin on 31 August 1943.

† George's brother Jim visited his sister Jeanne Sitter in Wilkie when he was home on leave.

‡ Ironically, Ken Bourne had been killed on operations on 13 August 1943.

down and saw Uncle George and Aunt Dais on the Sunday. I was planning on going to see Aunt Sally on the Monday morning but found our train left too early to go and see her.

I was planning on writing you as soon as we got back here but we operated both nights but we have tonight off, so at last I am getting the letter written. These jobs we do are the ones you hear over the radio when our night bombers have done something in strong force. I have been to the big place in Germany.* As you see, your son does get around.

That was nice for Jim to get up to see Jean.† It does seem to cut quite a bit off your leave, doesn't it?

I have had a couple of letters from Eldon Fleming since he came over here. He seems to be doing okay—he doesn't mind it over here. He had had a letter from Bill Smith and it seems Bill isn't very fussy about it.

Doug McMain seems quite happy and writes quite often. Ken Bourne hasn't written for some time but I guess he is okay.‡

It's too bad about what you thought of the pictures. Bill really isn't a beauty but he isn't a bad looking chap at all and really is a real man. Outside of our own family he is the best friend I've ever had in my life.

I just got a letter from you out of the mail now. Jim sure did seem to come and go quick. It is good he is looking so well. I'll bet you had a nice visit with him.

The news doesn't look too bad now, does it? You should have seen the people in London the afternoon the papers came out that Italy had quit—they were sure excited. We figured that meant we wouldn't have that long trip down there, but we came very close to it the other night anyway. The Alps sure looked pretty—it was bright moonlight and you could see everything. It seems funny, doesn't it? Two years ago I would have told anyone they were crazy if they had said I would see that.*

Well, Mom, I have to rush off again but I'm going to get this letter finished by tonight or my name isn't King.

Well, here goes again. I just went over to the office and told them I was going to write letters so he said okay. They are real good there. The one officer is a Canadian and is really nice.

I believe Norm is getting his commission now, so after he gets his I guess I will start trying to push mine. It takes them quite a while to get through.

I got the lilac fine, Mom. It is nice to have. I'm glad they were nice this year. I would have liked to have seen them. They never killed themselves blooming when I was home.

Well, Mom, this seems to be all I have to say for this time. I'm going to have to write a lot of letters now [that] I have time. I hope you are getting on okay with the harvest. I hope everyone is okay at home. I will write Dad a letter in a day or two.

> Love,
> George.

LETTER 51.

> R142247
> SGT. KING G.M.
> R.C.A.F. OVERSEAS
> September 19th, 1943

Hello Jim,

Well Old Cock, Old Cock, let me repeat Old Cock—emphasis on the cock. I have received two gruesome articles from you in the last week and now seize my pen in a blind rage and commence to write. I

* For another description of the flight over the Alps, see the excerpt from Doug Wylie's diary, page 152.

have just come off leave four days ago. Ripped off a couple of Ops. the first two nights I was back. Then had the mess dance (brawl), and am settling down to account for my long silence to several people.

Mom says you were home and very full in the face. They think it's fat, but I know what it is. Arf Arf Arf. By God, I've been waiting for a chance to spike you like that for ages, and now I've scored (Whizzard Prang).* Arf Arf.

We have made 9 journeys into the Hinterland, etc., and really blasted hell out of them. You sure wouldn't know this crew when they are on business and then see them in the pub.

I have a little W.A.A.F. just now that I can't bloody well get rid of. When we first came here she was supposed to be posted, so I thought what in hell can I lose and gave her the well-known shot for a couple of nights, and then damned if she didn't get the posting cancelled and now I'm really screwed. She chases hell out of me every time she sees me. I guess it is bloody well coming to me, but Jesus Christ, it gets tiresome.

We had a lovely brawl in our mess the other nite. I spent the last two hours of the nite trying to figure out if I was Napoleon or Dizzy Dean. My diet was whisky, gin, sherry, and hundreds of beers.

When I was on leave, Bill Baker and I went to Edinburough[sic] and then to Doug Wylie's brother's wedding in London, and then we whipped out to see Uncle George on Sunday and got God awful pissed in Henley. We had 2 1/2 gallons of beer each. I must admit I got rid of about a gallon of it on the way back to London. My supper departed with the gallon, but I still think we did well. Baker passed out when we were waiting to change trains, so I dragged him on the train and promptly passed out myself. We woke up in Paddington Station about an hour after the train had pulled in, so we staggered back to our hotel to sleep it off.

* "Wizard Prang" was contemporary RAF and even civilian slang for an extraordinary event, "wizard" meaning "extraordinary," and "prang" meaning "event." The phrase could be used in a number of ways. To "prang" an aircraft meant to crash it (see excerpt from Doug Wylie's diary on page 152), to "prang" a target meant to hit it with ordnance (see excerpt on page 149), and "wizard prang" could also be used to describe a particularly exciting operation (see excerpt on page 148).

Well, you old bugger, I guess this is all I have to say. Did you give any of the little locals a thrill while you were home? Aooooh! How was everything in the stable? Has little Harry's voice got any deeper, and how are Doc's habits?*

Your loving bro.,
George.

LETTER 52.

R142247
SGT. KING G.M.
R.C.A.F. OVERSEAS
September 20th, 1943

Dear Mom,

Here I am again. Nothing is new since I wrote three days ago. I seem to have caught up on most of my letters now. It is really getting cold here now. If you could get hold of a "V" necked sweater for me, it would really come in handy. It doesn't matter whether it has sleeves or not, but I want to wear it with my uniform, so it pretty well would have to have a V neck. The cigarettes and parcels don't seem to be getting here much these days, but there is always a letter from you every week and that is the main thing. We have our own aircraft now and it is getting its decoration today—no wall paper or anything, just a wolf painted on the outside. I guess I will be sending Jeannie a cable for her birthday pretty soon. I hope everyone is okay at home. Your busy season should be pretty well over by now. You seemed to be getting on pretty well. I got two "Suns" yesterday.

Love to all,
George.

* Harry and Doc were two of the workhorses on the farm.

OUR FILE... 46-14-X (CC(P)
REF. YOU...
DATED....

ROYAL CANADIAN AIR FORCE

September 28, 1943

Mr. W. King,
Summerberry, Sask.

Dear Mr. King:

      Word has been received at this Head-
quarters stating that your son, Sergeant George M.
King, is reported missing after air operations overseas
September 23.

      This word must have come as a great shock
and be the cause of the gravest anxiety.

      I sincerely hope that you can find consola-
tion in the fact that your son risked his life
willingly in the defence of freedom. What we all owe
to him is beyond estimation. During the anxious days
ahead may you be fortified by the spirit of courage and
hope which enabled him to discharge his duties, whatever
the cost.

      I earnestly pray that some information
regarding him will come through shortly. In the meanwhile,
may I commend you to Him, who is the Father of mercies and
God of all comfort.

      Yours sincerely,

         Hugh McFarlane
         Chaplain

      (H. McFarlane) Squadron Leader,
        for Air Officer Commanding,
    No. 2 Training Command, RCAF.,
         Winnipeg, Man.

R.C.A.F. G. 32
3500M—8-42 (2491)
H.Q. 885-G-32

LETTER 53.

C.P. Telegraphs
R.C.A.F. Casualties Officer
Ottawa, Ont.
September 25th, 1943

William King, Summerberry,

Regret to advise that your son R one four two two four seven Sergeant George McCowan King is reported missing after air operations overseas September twenty third. Letter follows.

R.C.A.F. Casualties Officer

LETTER 54.

C.P. Telegraphs
William King
Summerberry, Sask.
September 25th, 1943

LAC King J
R155809
4 Repair Depot
Scoudouc, N.B.

George reported missing twenty third.

Dad King

LETTER 55.

W.G. Oldbury
Wing Commander, Commanding
No. 218 (Gold Coast Squadron)
Royal Air Force
Downham Market, Norfolk, England
September 25th, 1943

Dear Mr. King,

I am writing to offer you the sincere sympathy both of myself and the whole Squadron in the anxiety you have experienced since learning that your son, Sgt. King G.M., is missing from air operations.

He was the navigator of an aircraft which took off to operate against the enemy on the night of 22/23rd September 1943, and the aircraft failed to return. Nothing has since been heard of it or of any of the crew.

There is a possibility that your son may have escaped from the aircraft by parachute, or in a forced landing in enemy territory, in which case he would be a Prisoner of War, and the news of this would not reach us for many weeks. The International Red Cross would be the first to receive any further news, and they would pass it immediately to Air Ministry. The Air Ministry would then communicate with you direct[ly], thus avoiding as much delay as possible.

I feel most deeply for you in this anxious time. If there is anything I can do to help, please let me know. We all join with you in hoping and praying that your son is safe.

Yours very sincerely,
W.G. Oldbury,
Wing Commander, Commanding,
No. 218 (Gold Coast) Squadron

LETTER 56.

Hugh McFarlane
Squadron Leader, Chaplain
No. 2 Training Command, RCAF
Winnipeg, Man.
September 28th, 1943

Dear Mr King,

Word has been received at this Headquarters stating that your son, Sergeant George M. King, is reported missing after air operations overseas September 23.

This word must have come as a great shock and be the cause of the gravest anxiety.

I sincerely hope that you can find consolation in the fact that your son risked his life willingly in the defence of freedom. What we all owe to him is beyond estimation. During the anxious days ahead may you be fortified by the spirit of courage and hope which enabled him to discharge his duties, whatever the cost.

I earnestly pray that some information regarding him will come through shortly. In the meanwhile, may I commend you to Him, who is the Father of mercies and God of all comfort.

Yours sincerely,
Hugh McFarlane
Squadron Leader,
Chaplain for Air Officer Commanding

LETTER 57.

CAN R132377
SGT. HEA R.W.
R.A.F.
R.C.A.F OVERSEAS
September 28, 1943

Dear Mrs. King,

By this time you probably know that George is missing. What I have to say will probably not make it any easier for you, but I do wish to tell you how sorry I am.

George & I were always the best of pals and many are the good times I've had at your place with him. He & I were together a couple of times on different stations, & I just arrived back at the same squadron as he was on the day after he went. To say the least I was dumbfounded. Plenty of fellows disappear on this job, but not until it is somebody you know & like does the fact come home to you.

George had done several operations over Germany, so he has had a lot to do with blasting the Nazis out of the war.

While I don't want to raise any false hope, there is always a good chance that he is a prisoner of war. As soon as I hear anything I will let you know.

Sincerely,
Riley Hea.

LETTER 58.

R155809
LAC KING J.
R.C.A.F.
Debert, N.S.
September 30, 1943

Dear Mother,

I received Dad's telegram with the terrible news last night. It was 4 1/2 days finding me, and had been recopied at Scoudouc and sent to Debert. I guess me not being permanent here caused the delay.

It's hard to believe that George is missing. I guess all we can do now is to pray for the best, and hope that he and the rest of the crew are still alive.

The poor fellow had been on operations for quite a while, he told me, but asked me not to tell you unless something happened. He thought you'd worry less that way. That was George all over, always thinking about the other person before himself.

I just couldn't get myself around to writing last night. If I'd received the telegram promptly, I would have let you know by telegram or sent a night letter, but decided it wasn't much use seeing it had gone so long.

I hope you get some better news soon. Did they send you any particulars or anything? At least there's still some hope.

I received a letter from you yesterday, also forwarded from Scoudouc, and was sorry to hear about Dad's heart. He'll have to be real careful, and be sure not to over-exert himself.

I guess the harvesting will be pretty well on by now.

This is about all I can write tonight. Hoping to hear some better news soon. I wish I could be with you, as I know how terrible you all feel.

> Your loving son,
> Jim.

LETTER 59.

> C8554
> S/L W.J. Bell
> Chaplain (P)
> RCAF OVERSEAS
> October 1st, 1943

Dear Mr King,

It was with a great deal of regret that I learned that your son George was reported missing from flying operations on the 22/23rd of September.

This will be a hard blow to you and the folks at home and my sympathy goes out to you. The days ahead will be filled with great anxiety, hoping for the best, yet dreading in your heart the very worst. I pray that your worst fears will not be realized but that somewhere George and his comrades may be safe.

As you are no doubt aware, it takes time for news to come the regular way from occupied territory, but you may rest assured that everything that is humanly possible is being done to that end. I trust that it will not be long before you hear again.

Meantime it is also my hope that you will be finding comfort and strenghth[sic] in your faith and in the knowledge that God does care for us and for ours. Religion does not promise that life will be easy for us, but it does promise that with our faith in God and "in the ultimate decency of things" we can triumph over all circumstances, even those that are bitter and tragic. May such a faith be yours in these dreadful days.

If there is anything I can do, please do not hesitate to write. I knew George and was talking with him not so very long ago. We had a common bond. He came from Summerberry and I from Lloydminster where my family now reside. I was minister of the United Church there before I came into the service. We had quite a talk together.

May God Bless you all at home.

> Yours Very Sincerely,
> W.J. Bell, Squadron Leader
> Chaplain

LETTER 60.

> George King
> 50 Mount View
> Henley-on-Thames
> Oxon., England
> October 1st, 1943

Dear Bill and Agnes,

I have just received your cable about George and can't tell you how sorry I am but I had heard from Headquarters the same day and have had a letter from his Wing Commander who gives a little hope that the crew bailed out or made a forced landing but of course they would be prisoners of war. Let us hope it is so. Of course I have let Dais know and she was writing to Sally. She sends her deepest regrets and hopes we shall hear better news. George and all of us had got [to be] such good pals when he came on his short leaves. I don't think I can say more. Hoping we shall hear some tidings of him, and hope for the best. With love to you both and hope to find you both well I remain

Your loving brother,
George

LETTER 61.

Sallie King
55 Shirlock Road
Hampstead N.W.
London, England
October 3rd, 1943

My dear Will & Agnes,

I can't tell you how it hurts me to write this to you, & how I wish it was all a dream. I know how you all loved the dear boy, as we all did. He seemed as if he had always been amongst us. Poor old George is very upset & he had been to see him for a few hours & he was so looking forward to seven days leave & he was coming to see me. How wicked it all seems but we must hope for the best. He may have escaped & [been] taken prisoner. That is dreadful but there would be just a possibility of seeing him again. There has[sic] been a good many come home again. We must leave it all in God's hands & hope for the best. Try & not fret, my dears.

I should like to hear from you to know how you all are & if you get any news. George was writing to you & Daisy wrote to me. It was a shock to them all. Please give my love to Jennie & I hope she is well & Bruce. I am expecting a letter from her. She was going to send me some snaps, but the mail is such a long time coming now. I hope Bill

& Jim are well. Do write to me soon & let me know how you all are & if there should be any news.

There is nothing much to write about. Daisy & Kathleen came up for the day a few Sundays ago, but they had to go back early because of the black-out. They were very well then & young Tom keeps fairly well & is able to do his fire watching, which is a blessing.

Now my dear brother & sister, I hope to hear from you soon. God bless you all & keep you safe. With my fondest love & sympathy.

> From your loving Sister,
> Sallie

P.S. Lottie sends her love.

LETTER 62.

> W.R. Gunn, Flight Lieutenant
> R.C.A.F. Casualties Officer
> For Chief of the Air Staff
> Royal Canadian Air Force
> Ottawa, Ontario
> October 6th, 1943

Mr. William King,
Summerbury[sic] Saskatchewan.

Dear Mr. King,

It is my painful duty to confirm the telegram recently received by you which informed you that your son, Sergeant George McGowan[sic] King, is reported missing on Active Service.

Advice has been received from the Royal Canadian Air Force Casualties Officer, Overseas, that your son was a member of the crew of an aircraft which failed to return to its base after air operations over Hanover, Germany, on the night of September 22nd and early morning of September 23rd, 1943. There were four other members of the Royal Canadian Air Force in the crew, and they also have been reported missing. Since you may wish to know their names and next-of-kin we are listing them below:

Pilot Officer R.F. Eberle,
Next-of-kin, Mr. Fred Eberle (father)
127 Eastwood Road, Toronto, Ontario

Sergeant N.V. Spencer,
Next-of-kin, Mrs. N.V. Spencer (wife)
3963 West, 12th Avenue,
Vancouver, B.C.

Sergeant D.M. Wylie,
Next-of-kin, Mrs. D.M. Wylie (wife)
118 Glenview Ave., Toronto, Ontario

Sergeant A.W. Baker,
Next-of-kin, Mr. A.W. Baker (father)
121 Melville Avenue, Toronto, Ontario

This does not necessarily mean that your son has been killed or wounded. He may have landed in enemy territory and might be a Prisoner of War. Enquires[sic] have been made through the International Red Cross Society and all other appropriate sources and you may be assured that any further inforamation[sic] received will be communicated to you immediately.

Your son's name will not appear on the official casualty list for five weeks. You may, however, release to the Press or Radio the fact that he is reported missing, but not disclosing the date, place or his unit.

May I join with you and Mrs. King in the hope that better news will be forthcoming in the near future.

Yours sincerely,

M. Cameron A/S/O

for W.R. Gunn, Flight Lieutenant

R.C.A.F. Casualties Officer

for Chief of the Air Staff

LETTER 63.

Mrs E. Morement
40 Trower Street
Frenchwood
Preston Lanes
Lancashire, England
October 10th, 1943

Dear Mr King,

I write to you as a mother to a father expressing my deepest sympathy in the anxious time of waiting for news of our dear lads reported missing from night operations. My only son was Flight Engineer on your son's aircraft, and I should like you to know my son's opinion of all the crew. He said they were the finest bunch of lads one could wish to meet. Their grand comradeship, friendliness, and the knowledge of one another's ability to carry out any duty allotted to them made them second to none on the station. He thought his five Canadian pals were the best in the world. I am convinced they have either parachuted down or made a forced landing and at the worst [are] prisoners of war. I trust and pray earnestly that we shall see our loved ones as soon as this terrible war is ended.

Yours sincerely,
Mrs E. Morement

LETTER 64.

Arnold McQuoid*
Guelph, Ontario
October 17th, 1943

Dear Mrs. and Mr. King,

You will no doubt be surprised at receiving a letter from me, but I thought I might be able to help a little by writing and telling you of some cases I know of, just like yours.

Mother wrote and told me that you had received word that George was missing, & Mrs. King, I am sorry. But I really didn't write just to say I was sorry, Mrs. King, but rather to try & explain just how much hope there really is. You must know that after every operation over enemy territory, a number of our boys fail to come back, but a large percentage of those have been taken prisoner. The day I received word of George, the fellow I work with received word, after waiting for three months, that his brother was a prisoner of war & quite safe.

We have at our station what we call the Intelligence room. In this room we have boards of information brought back from enemy camps by escaped prisoners, and although the Germans have a very bad

* Arnold McQuoid was a serviceman who was originally from the Summerberry area. For most of the war, he was a wireless instructor at No. 4 Wireless School in Guelph, Ontario. After the war, he worked as a pharmacist in Wolseley, Saskatchewan.

name, they do treat their prisoners with a fair amount of civility. You probably have seen a lot of movie pictures showing how inhumane German officers are to our boys, but I can assure you, Mrs. King, that this is eighty percent propaganda. I have even spoken with men who have returned—by that I mean escaped from German prison camps— & although life is not of the very best, it is still a lot better than some of the pictures we have painted for us here in Canada.

I feel so terribly helpless myself, sitting here in Canada with a nice soft-cushioned job. I would give my right arm to get over & do a bit of the fighting myself, but so far I have had to remain behind. I may get my chance yet, though, & I pray God that if I ever do, I may take full advantage of it.

I don't know whether I have said what I meant to say in this letter or not, but hope & pray, Mrs. King, & God will do the rest.

> Sincerely,
> Arnold McQuoid.

LETTER 65.

> Annie Taylor
> Pinkham, Sask.
> October 19th, 1943

Dear Agnes,

I was so relieved to get your letter. It was kind of you to write so soon. Georgie and Jennie were saying how hard you & Will were trying to hold up, but at such a cost. No wonder you wonder is life worth while.

What a nice letter you got from the Wing Commander so

promptly. And wasn't that a lovely letter from Riley Hea? I had already decided that George had gone down over Hanover, and just think how many even since then are missing, whatever the cost. Riley Hea's letter seems to bring home to me afresh the thoughts of those young boys when a comrade does not return.

Yes, I had the snaps already[sic] to return at the wrong time. I kept them a little while to show as almost every day I seem to have some mother in and they all seem so hungry for news and pictures. 2 women mentioned that they were going to write and ask their son for a picture of his whole crew.

When [I was] in to see lawyer Tracy of K'dsly* a few days ago, he told me that his wife's brother who has been missing for 14 months has just turned up a prisoner in Germany. He had written many letters and they are only now getting through. He is well in every way and wrote such a good letter that Tracy went across the street to let me see it, but his wife was out & had the door locked.

We hope to have Jennie & Bruce along some Sunday soon. Mrs. Evans and Thelma were lonely in their own home, and Thelma thinks Jean is great. She looks so much better. How I wish Jean lived at Kindersley. Now with gas and tires we can't meet often,† whereas a few years ago we could have met every six weeks.

I am going to write to James tonight, too. I know how hard it will be for him. He & George always had their arms around each other when I was there as they went off across the field. Poor Bill, too, thought such a lot of George.

Four men are here talking to Ernest. They were working at the church today. Mrs. Ross called in a few minutes [ago] to say goodbye. She is going to the Calgary clinic to have a kidney removed. I never saw anyone so thin.

* "K'dsly" refers to the town of Kindersley, near Pinkham, Saskatchewan.

† Gasoline and rubber were rationed during the war, something which limited the mobility of people throughout North America and Europe.

Gram. says she must give that rascal Ernest a talking to as he is getting forgetful. Forgot a loaf of bread for her again tonight.

With love,
Annie

LETTER 66.

R155809
LAC KING J.
R.C.A.F.
SCOUDOUC, N.B.
October 25th, 1943

Dear Mother,

It's 8 days since I wrote last, but I intended writing sooner, but it's been about the busiest 8 days I ever spent. I've been to both St. John and Debert, and back again. We didn't have much to do at St. John, as the plane was in good shape. Then the day I got back from there I was sent to Debert. The planes there were all fixed up and loaded on trailers, and I went down to help the driver of one of the trucks. We were 2 days coming back—in fact, we just got in about 2 hrs ago. It rained all the time, and the roads were in very poor shape, especially the dirt ones.

I had 3 letters when I got back tonight and 2 Wolseley News. One letter was from you and Dad, and one was from George, written Sept. 19th. I was glad to get it, but it really took the spirit out of me for a while. He told me about his trip to Henley, the wedding, etc., and also he'd been over Germany 9 times, so no matter what has happened to him, he sure got a few good cracks at the Nazis. The way he put it, he said "they'd really blasted hell out of them."

I just got back in time for a real panic. They decided to put everyone that worked in a certain section together in a certain barracks, like our section all in one building, and another section in another, so practically every man at the station had to "pick up his bed and walk." Hanning was in an awful way when I arrived, as he was just starting to move himself. Benham, Harnett and I—he wasn't going to let us get separated and we were all away but him. However, I arrived in time to help. It's really better the way it is, as now everybody in the room works in the same hangar. The four of us have bunks right together. The salvage section was first on the station over the top in the victory loan. They raffled off two $50 bonds in our section for 50c a ticket. I had tickets on both, but didn't win, of course. P.A. Yeast* from Maple Creek won one, and Hanning won the other. Boy he was excited, especially as he's of a very excitable nature.

Bob Moore and Geo. Belquist are both back off leave now. George is in our barracks too, but Bob doesn't work in salvage, so he's in another building. So the place seems more like home now.

Hub. Kent† got posted to Yarmouth. Gosh he was mad—just him and one other guy that he hardly knew, and nobody cares much for. I shook hands with him before I left for Debert and said maybe we'd be down that way on temp. duty some time and see him. He said, "I hope they send a crew down there for the whole winter," so you can tell how he felt. It was really a crime as he'd been here 2 yrs and knew all the fellows in the section. Then to get sent away alone. He'll probably be promoted to Sgt. right away, but that still didn't console him.

This truck driver from Candiac came to me quite excited. There's a WAAF from Lemberg on this station, and I was to look her up. But Smith the fellow who worked for Rod Christie‡ had done as Romanow (Slabiak's cousin) had wanted him to do, and reports she speaks quite

* P.A. "Speed" Yeast was a serviceman from Maple Creek, and was best man at the wedding of Geoffrey Strudwick of Pilot Butte, a friend of James's.

† "Hub" Kent was a serviceman from the Summerberry district.

‡ Rod Christie owned a farm near Grenfell.

broken English. I guess that's what enthused the guy so much.

I see by the news that Olive is married—also Marguerite McMain.* The funny thing was when I was at home a couple of years ago they seemed to be very deeply in love with each other.

There doesn't seem to be much more to say. Oh yes, in the news it said Mrs. W.E. Taylor of Pinkham had been visiting relatives in the district. That can't be right, can it, as you've never mentioned it? Also, Mrs. Bruce "Setter" had been there. I had a letter from Jeannie since she went back.

Well, I guess I'll have to close now, and will write sooner next time, but when you're on the road, you can't very well write, as quite often we travel most of the night. There are only certain places that can accomodate[sic] a gang of men, and you have to get to those places. I've stayed in Amherst, Springhill, and Parrsboro overnight in the last week, so you can see how we've been moving. Bob Moore says every time he sees me I'm either heading towards the hangar or the barracks with my club bag, but maybe we'll get a little rest now. But Sgt. Simpson is back and he may want me to go out again.

> Your loving son,
> Jim.

P.S. I have those pictures of George's crew with me. The only one I left was the one of George alone.

* The Olives lived near Summerberry. Marguerite McMain married Donald Markham in 1943.

LETTER 67.

W.G. Oldbury
Wing Commander, Commanding
No. 218 (Gold Coast Squadron)
Royal Air Force
Downham Market
Norfolk, England
October 30th, 1943

Dear Mrs. King,

I am in receipt of your letter dated October 10th, 1943. All parcels addressed to R.C.A.F. personnel who become missing are returned to the Canadian Overseas Depot. After receiving your letter, I wrote to Canadian Overseas Postal Depot asking them to re-address any parcels for Sergeant King to his uncle. I received a reply today to the effect that civilians in England cannot be accepted as alternative addressees for parcels for members of the R.C.A.F. who have been reported missing.

One parcel addressed to Sergeant King with O.C. 218 Squadron as the alternative addressee containing shoes I still have. These shoes could be sold to one of the Air Crew of the Squadron and the money placed in the 218 (Gold Coast) Squadron Comforts Fund or credited to Sergeant King's account. Kindly let me know what you wish me to do.

Yours sincerely,
W.G. Oldbury
Wing Commander, Commanding
No. 218 (Gold Coast) Squadron

LETTER 68.

Kathryn Spencer
3963 West 12th Avenue
Vancouver, B.C.
November 4th, 1943

Dear Mrs. King,

Just a note to tell you that we've had a wire from Mrs. Doug Wylie in Toronto saying that Billie Baker, the rear gunner of the crew, has been reported a prisoner of war.

Gosh, isn't that wonderful news? Ours will be next, so keep hoping and praying.

Love,
Kathryn Spencer*

* Kathryn Spencer was the widow of Norman Spencer, the pilot in George's crew.

ROYAL CANADIAN AIR FORC

CHAPLAIN SERVICES

R.C
Nov

Mr. W. King,
SUMMERBERRY, Sask.

Dear Mr. King:

You will no doubt have received the news that y̶[ ]̶ missing on the 22nd of September, is now believed to have been killed in action.

I know the sorrow that will prevail in you hearts on the receipt of this news and I am deeply sympathetic. It does seem so final doesn't it and ends the hope that would exist in your minds that your son might still be alive. I was hoping too that the next letter I would write to you would be to join with you in thanksgiving that George had turned up somewhere safe and sound, but evidently it wasn't to be.

I had an Airmail from his Aunt, Mrs. McCowan, enquiring about him and asking for more particulars. Unfortunately I have no more information than has been relayed to you and I am quite sure if the casualty branch had anything to offer further, they would do so. I knew George's Aunt, Mrs. McCowan when I was at Yorkton as I had the unfortunate task of burying her boy when he was killed there. Would you be good enough to pass on the word to her that I received her letter and that there is nothing to add to what you already know.

I do pray that God will give you His strength at this time to bear this tragic burden and keep alive in you heart a burning hope for the future, for there is a future, whether it be here or hereafter God will vindicate His own word and make all things, even the bitter things, work together for good. May there be given to you and yours the comfort and the assurance that comes from His own word in this matter.

One thing is worth holding on to and that is that George belongs now to a great company who have enriched the world by their magnificent sacrifice. Free people everywhere, lifted out of their bondage and suffering, must thank God for boys like yours who have given all they had, to purchase that freedom. The price is heavy we know, and will be heavier yet, but I know none who pay it more cheerfully than these very fine boys over here. Its an inspiration to watch them and I can say quite truthfully there are none that I know of who would want to get out of it. Whatever happens to them I don't know, but they seem to be lifted above desire for personal safety and go on with the job, that has to be done with a quiet courageous efficiency that is astounding. I went through the last war and I haven't seen anything like it. Its a pity that such fine lads have to give their lives but you may be sure that while they live they live, packing into a few short years experiences that are rich and full.

I do pray that you will not sorrow as those without hope and that in the days that are to come you will have reason to be quietly proud in your own heart that you had such a son and that you had such a cause to give him to.

Yours very sincerely,

W. Bell sh

Chapter 4:

"Killed in Action"

LETTER 69.

C.P. Telegraphs
R.C.A.F. Casualties Officer
Royal Canadian Air Force
Ottawa, Ontario
November 14th, 1943

William King, Summerberry, Sk.,

Regret to advise International Red Cross quoting German information states your son Sergeant George McCowan King lost his life September twenty second but does not give additional particulars. Pending further confirmation your son is to be considered missing believed killed. Please accept my sincere sympathy. Letter following.

R.C.A.F. Casualties Officer

LETTER 70.

C.P. Telegraphs
Mae Wylie*
Toronto, Ont.
November 16th, 1943

Wm. King, Summerberry:

Sgt. Doug Wylie reported killed. Have you received any word about George? Please wire immediately collect.

Love,
Mae Wylie

* Mae Wylie was the widow of Doug Wylie, the bomb aimer in George's crew.

134

LETTER 71.

C.P. Telegraphs
William King
Summerberry, Sask.
November 17th, 1943

Mae Wylie, Toronto:

We mourn with you. Sorry. George also reported killed.

Love,
Wm. King

LETTER 72.

James G. Gardiner*
Minister of Agriculture
Ottawa, Ontario
November 18th, 1943

William King, Esq.,
Summerbury[sic], Sask.

Dear Mr. King,

I regret to note your son's name in the casualty list which appeared in the press recently.

It is the earnest prayer of Mrs. Gardiner and me that the anxiety which will be yours through a report that he is missing will end in the good news that he is alive even if a prisoner. We realise from following the lists that a very considerable percentage of those missing escape or turn up as prisoners of war.

We hope with you that this will be your experience.

Yours sincerely,
James G. Gardiner

* James Gardiner, former premier of Saskatchewan from the town of Lemberg, approximately 40 kilometres north of Summerberry, was certainly able to empathise with the families of servicemen killed at war. Two of his brothers had been killed in the First World War, and for a time he was minister of National War Services under Prime Minister William Lyon Mackenzie King during the Second World War. While he served as federal minister of Agriculture, Gardiner learned that his oldest son Edwin, an RCAF fighter pilot, had been killed at Dieppe in August of 1942. Stricken by grief at the death of her son, Gardiner's wife Violet committed suicide in 1944, herself becoming what Gardiner termed a "war casualty" (Ward and Smith, *Jimmy Gardiner*, 249).

LETTER 73.

Sallie King
55 Shirlock Road
Hampstead N.W.
London, England
November 19th, 1943

My dear Agnes & Will,

Thank you so much for your letter. I really don't know what to say to you both in your trouble & anxiety about your dear boy, George, & I do hope please God that he is safe & well, somewhere. We must all hope for the best. Poor old George is very cut up. They saw a great deal of him at Henley, & Daisy & all the young people took to him. They all thought him such a lovely boy & so affectionate to them all. I only saw him the once, but was expecting him, as he was due for a 7 days' leave. He did try to come to see me when he came up to London for a wedding, but couldn't get away from the crew, but he managed to get down to see George & took one of the crew with him. He was quite one of the family. They will miss his visits, but we will hope to see him again.

I must thank you for being so kind to send me some stockings. I don't suppose I shall ever get them, but thank you for your kind thought, & I am sure Daisy will think the same. I sent your letter to her.

Give my love to Will. I should so love to get a letter from him & Jennie too & how is she? It was nice for you to have her home to cheer you all up. I do hope Bill & Jim are well. Do you see much of Jim? I suppose he is a long way away from you. We are all getting so tired of this dreadful war. We are having such a lot of raids again, & we can never fully undress in case of getting up in the night, &

everything is so quiet—no one about & all blacked out.

Well my dears, I do hope you are keeping well & don't fret & we will hope all will be well soon. I hope you will write as soon as you can or hear any news. With my fondest love to you all, & hope you will all be together at Xmas. Lottie sends her love & sympathy.

> From ever your loving Sister,
> Sallie

LETTER 74.

> Vera Patterson
> Summerberry, Sask.
> November 19th 1943

Dear Mrs King,

On behalf of the "Ladies Aid" I would like to extend to you our deepest sympathy at this time, and we hope and pray that God will give you strength to bear your great loss.

> Your Sorrowing Friend,
> Vera Patterson

LETTER 75.

> Nessie Baker
> 121 Melville Avenue
> Toronto, Ontario
> November 21st, 1943

Dear Mrs King,

We have just received your letter telling us about George, and our hearts go out to you and your family in your sad loss.

I am sorry that we are not closer to you because I think I could be some comfort to you on account of Bill and George being together and knowing each other so well.

We seem to be living in rather a unique time. While some are rejoicing, others are in sorrow. However, as you say in your letter, you know that George would feel proud to think he had done his part for humanity.

I have been in touch with Mrs Eberle and Mrs Wylie and they have both received word from Ottawa that Ray and Doug have been killed. To me this whole thing is a tragedy, and nothing I can say could express my feelings.

We have had further word from Ottawa regarding Bill. He is in the hospital with a fractured skull and a broken upper arm. Under ordinary circumstances this would be alarming but I cannot help but feel that he has been fortunate when I think of what happened to his pals.

We are naturally hoping that he is getting along alright, and just can't wait to hear from him, although if his right arm is broken it will be some time before he will be able to write.

If I get any further word, I will keep you informed. If it is any comfort for you to know, we still remember you and George in our prayers because I have found that their[sic] is nothing more comforting than that.

As you say in your letter, let us hope that it won't be long before this terrible ordeal is over and that the world may be able to settle down and live in peace.

Yours sincerely,
Nessie Baker.*

* This letter is signed by Nessie Baker, the mother of Air Gunner Bill Baker, but it appears to have actually been composed and written by someone else. The handwriting, grammatical style, and use of the word "and" rather than the ampersand do not match that of her later letter, one in which she apologises for not having written sooner. In her later letter, she says that health problems and the shock of hearing that her son had gone missing had kept her from writing, and so someone—perhaps a daughter—must have written this letter in her stead.

LETTER 76.

C8554
S/L W.J. Bell
Chaplain (P)
RCAF OVERSEAS
November 21st, 1943

Dear Mr. King,

You will no doubt have received the news that your son George, reported missing on the 22nd of September, is now believed to have been killed in action.

I know the sorrow that will prevail in you[r] hearts on the receipt of this news, and I am deeply sympathetic. It does seem so final, doesn't it, and ends the hope that would exist in your minds that your son might still be alive. I was hoping too that the next letter I would write to you would be to join with you in thanksgiving that George had turned up somewhere safe and sound, but evidently it wasn't to be.

I had an Airmail from his Aunt, Mrs. McCowan, enquiring about him and asking for more particulars. Unfortunately I have no more information than has been relayed to you and I am quite sure if the casualty branch had anything to offer further, they would do so. I knew George's Aunt, Mrs. McCowan, when I was at Yorkton as I had the unfortunate task of burying her boy when he was killed there. Would you be good enough to pass on the word to her that I received her letter and that there is nothing to add to what you already know?

I do pray that God will give you His strength at this time to bear this tragic burden and keep alive in you[r] heart a burning hope for the future, for if there is a future, whether it be here or hereafter,

God will vindicate His own word and make all things, even the bitter things, work together for good. May there be given to you and yours the comfort and the assurance that comes from His own word in this matter.

One thing is worth holding on to and that is that George belongs now to a great company who have enriched our world by their magnificent sacrifice. Free people everywhere, lifted out of their bondage and suffering, must thank God for boys like yours who have given all they had to purchase that freedom. The price is heavy, we know, and will be heavier yet, but I know none who pay it more cheerfully than these very fine boys over here. It's an inspiration to watch them, and I can say quite truthfully there are none that I know of who would want to get out of it. Whatever happens to them I don't know, but they seem to be lifted above desire for personal safety and go on with the job that has to be done with a quiet, courageous efficiency that is astounding. I went through the last war and I haven't seen anything like it. It's a pity that such fine lads have to give their lives, but you may be sure that while they live, they live, packing into a few short years experiences that are rich and full.

I do pray that you will not sorrow as those without hope, and that in the days that are to come, you will have reason to be quietly proud in your own heart that you had such a son and that you had such a cause to give him to.

Yours very sincerely,
W.J. Bell, Squadron Leader
Chaplain

LETTER 77.

R.C.A.F. Casualties Officer
Royal Canadian Air Force
Ottawa, Ontario
November 22nd, 1943

Dear Mr. King,

Confirming my telegram of recent date, I regret to inform you that the Royal Canadian Air Force Casualties Officer Overseas advises me that a report has been received from the International Red Cross Society at Geneva, concerning your son, Flight Sergeant George McCowan King, previously reported missing on Active Service.

The report quotes German information which states that your son lost his life on September 22nd, 1943, but does not contain any further particulars. The International Red Cross is making every effort to obtain the location of your son's grave. However, I feel sure you will appreciate the difficulties attendant upon securing additional details.

Since this information originates from enemy sources it is necessary for the present to consider your son "missing believed killed" until confirmed by further evidence. However, in the absence of additional information, his death will be presumed after a lapse of six months from the date he was reported missing.

May I assure you and Mrs. King of my deepest sympathy.

Yours sincerely,
M.M. Campbell, A/S/O
for W.R. Gunn,
Squadron Leader, R.C.A.F. Casualties Officer,
for Chief of the Air Staff

LETTER 78.

The Hea Family
Grand Coulee, Sask.
November 22nd, 1943

Dear Mr. and Mrs. King,

    It was with much sorrow we learned of the loss of your dear son George. Words cannot express what we feel for you in our hearts. Riley feels the loss of his friend very much, & his letters home are sad.

    To you all we send our deepest sympathy.
    The Hea family

LETTER 79.

Estates Branch
Ottawa, Canada
November 24, 1943

Mrs. Wm. King,
Summerbury[sic], Saskatchewan
Re: King, G. McC., Sgt. (Missing)
No. R142247, R.C.A.F.

    The enclosed letter addressed to you was located in the personal effects of the above named whom it is regretted is presently missing on Active Service.*

    This letter is sent on to you as we know he would have wished you to have it.
    N.O. Seagram, S/Ldr.,
    For L.M. Firth, Lt. Col.,
    Administrator of Estates.

    Encl.

* The enclosed letter is not extant.

LETTER 80.

Estates Branch
Ottawa, Canada
November 24, 1943

Miss Patricia Kerr*
285 Angus Cres.,
Regina, Sask.
Re: King, G. McC., Sgt. (Missing)
No. R142247, R.C.A.F.

The enclosed letters addressed to you were located in the personal effects of the above named whom it is regretted is presently missing on Active Service.†

These letters are sent on to you as we know he would have wished you to have them.

N.O. Seagram, S/Ldr.,

For L.M. Firth, Lt. Col.,

Administrator of Estates.

Encl.

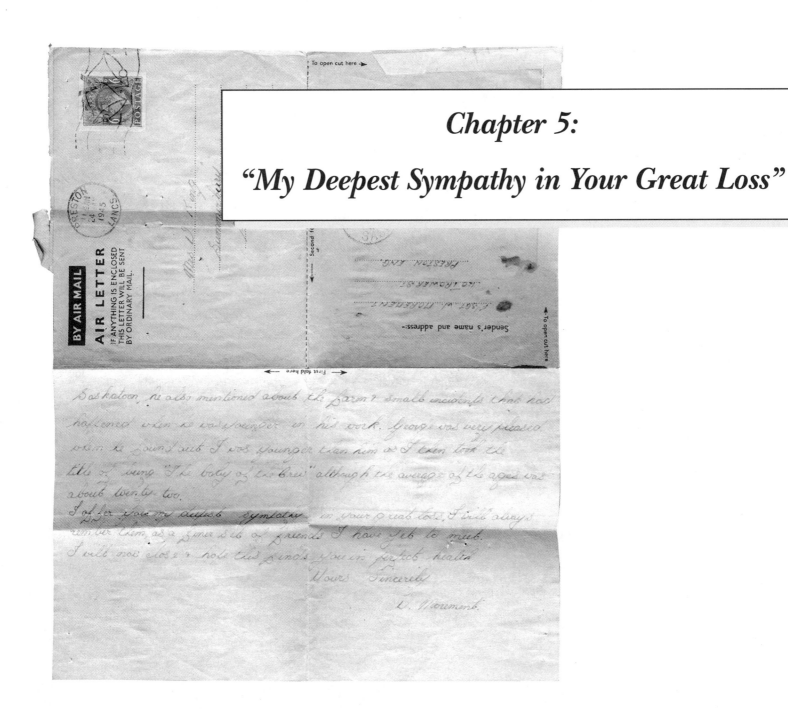

Chapter 5:

"My Deepest Sympathy in Your Great Loss"

Saskatoon, he also mentioned about the farm & small incidents that had happened when he was younger in his work. George was very pleased when he found out I was younger than him as I then took the title of being "The baby of the crew" although the average of the ages was about twenty two.

I offer you my deepest sympathy in your great loss, I will always remember them as a finer set of friends I have yet to meet.

I will now close & hope this finds you in perfect health.

Yours Sincerely

D. Warriment

Summerberry Boy Listed As Killed

Once again war came very near to this district when word was received on Sunday from the War Office advising the parents of Srgt. Obs. George King that Geneva Red Cross had reported him killed in a raid over Hanover, Germany, on the night of Sept. 22.

George McCowan King was born at Summerberry on April 19th, 1922. He graduated from the Summerberry High school and in Nov. 1941 enlisted in the R.C.A.F. He took his training at Paulson, Regina, and obtained his wings at Pearce. He went overseas in Dec. 1942 and took further training until June when he commenced flying over Germany and Italy.

On Sept 22nd during the big raid his bombing plane, a Sterling[sic], with a crew of seven, failed to return and word was received listing the crew as missing. A later message reported one of the gunners a prisoner of war in Germany and hopes were entertained that if one was a prisoner all would eventually be reported so. However, wires have been received by parents of two of the boys notifying them that their sons were war casualties.

George was a young man who was a general favorite in the community. Of a kindly, quiet nature, he made many friends who deeply regret the passing of one who took an active part in all sports and who was a general favorite with everyone.

He leaves, besides his parents, a sister, Mrs. Bruce Sitter of Wilkie, and two brothers, James, RCAF, of Scoudouc, N.B., and Bill on the farm. To these sorrowing relatives the sympathy of the entire community is extended.

LETTER 81.

Mae Wylie
118 Glenview Avenue
Toronto, Ontario
November 25, 1943

Dear Mrs. King,

For some time I have intended writing you but I know you'll understand just why I haven't.

This is a very anxious and trying time for us all. Although Ottawa hasn't given us much hope for the boys I still cling to my strong feeling that they are all alright somewhere. I am sure you must feel the same way.

I suppose you already know that two of the boys are Prisoners of War, one of them being an R.A.F. boy. I hope for Mrs. Hicks' sake that it is her husband that is the other Prisoner as she has a two year old son.

Mrs. Baker has probably told you that we have visited together. I have also talked to the Eberle family but haven't as yet seen them. It seems so difficult to do all the things you should in these times.

My brother-in-law just returned from overseas a couple of weeks ago and he had been on Doug's station before leaving the country and was able to get his diary for me. It certainly is very interesting reading and one day I plan to type out parts of it and send to the families of the different boys. Newt* met your son George on a couple of different occassions[sic] and said he thought he was a grand boy. He said that the whole crew were a swell bunch and I have heard that more than once. It is nice to know that they liked each other so much and got on together in such a co-operative way.

* Newton Wylie was Doug Wylie's brother, and also served overseas.

I still believe that we haven't sufficient information to give up hope. You read about so many different cases where families have received the same word as we have and they turn up. There is still a good chance that our boys will.

In the meantime while we are awaiting further news, I'll be thinking of you and your husband because I know what you are going through.

When you are feeling like writing I would really like to hear from you.

Sincerely,
Mae Wylie.

Excerpts from Doug Wylie's diary*

Monday, August 23, 1943. We took more lectures today—a real gen† one from Sq./Ldr. Saunders, our Flight Commander. He is taking Normie along as second Pilot tonite to Berlin so it looks as tho' Normie is going to have a hot old time. He went out of here tonite looking a little white and I don't blame him.

Tuesday, August 24, 1943. Normie got back okay and enjoyed his trip to Berlin—"Wizard Prang." Jerry was over here last nite and dropped a 1000 pounder on the runway and about 70 anti-personal[sic] butterfly bombs. The bomb demolition squad has been setting them off all day. They sure make a racket. We did a D.I. (Daily Inspection) on "U" Uncle this afternoon and we are going to use it tonite.

Wednesday, August 25, 1943. We did our first "OP." as a crew here last nite with a mine laying trip to the Frisian Islands. Too bad all "OPS." aren't that easy. We are on again tonite—the same thing only longer. We did our D.I.'s this morning on "U" Uncle again. We have briefing at five tonite so we have been rushing all day.

* Mae Wylie typed out this excerpt from her husband's diary and sent it to Agnes in a later letter which is not extant. For the purposes of continuity, however, I include it here after her letter in which she promises to send it.

† "Gen" as used here was RAF slang for "informational."

Thursday, August 26, 1943. Our mining trip last nite was 6 1/2 hours. We laid them off the North of the River leading to Bordeaux. We saw all kinds of flak and searchlights, especially at Nantes, but we didn't have a shot fired at us. Didn't see any fighters. We have tonite off at last.

Friday, August 27, 1943. Cold as "hell" today with a steady drizzle. We have been informed that we are on "OPS." tonite, so I guess this is the real thing this time. We don't know what the target is yet, but will find out at briefing at 5. P.M. The target is Nuremburg[sic].

Saturday, August 28, 1943. We took off last night but just got off when our port inner engine exhaust broke and on orders we jettisoned in the Wash* and landed with three engines. Everybody marvelled at the landing Normie made. We were 3000 lbs. over the maximum for landing. Thirty-three kites are missing from the raid—two out of ten from here.

Sunday, August 29, 1943. We had a stand down today so we just did our daily inspections on the kite and fooled around all day. I am dead tired so am going to bed early tonite.

Monday, August 30, 1943. We are on "OPS." tonite. We have been getting things ready all day. We have just finished briefing and we are going to Munchan Gladback[sic], a city about ten miles west of Dusseldorf in "Happy Valley."† We aren't taking off until twelve o'clock—this looks like it will be fun.

Tuesday, August 31, 1943. Quite a show last nite! All kinds of flak, searchlights and fighters. We weren't attacked, but we saw lots of attacks and three kites blown to bits over the target. It was one huge mass of fires and I don't think we will have to go back. We are on again tonite—this time to Berlin. Everybody feels rather apprehensive. Frank Middleton is missing, also another crew. 28 lost.

Wednesday, September 1, 1943. Well, now we have Berlin on our log books. We didn't get back until 4:30, giving us 8 hours, 15 minutes in the air. It was rather nerve wracking. We saw planes being shot down by fighters all around us, but we didn't have any attacks. We really pranged the target. Lots of fires. There was a lot of cloud that kept the searchlights off us. We saw a fighter

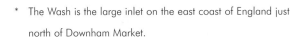

*   The Wash is the large inlet on the east coast of England just north of Downham Market.

†   "Happy Valley" was a nickname for the Ruhr Valley in Germany.

over the target. Only the Wing Commander is missing from here, but we lost 47 altogether. We had a hole in one gas tank.

Thursday, September 2, 1943. We were given our own kite today. It is brand new and won't be ready for a while as they are putting in various "OPS." equipment. We took all the guns out and brought them into the gun cleaning room. We have been working on them all day. They are a mass of greece[sic]. I am dead tired again. Going to bed early.

Friday, September 3, 1943. We did fighter affiliation today, but the kite we were using had something wrong with the elevators and Normie had a tough time controlling it, so after the Hurricane made a couple of attacks we washed it out as we couldn't beat him under those conditions. Dead tired, getting to bed early.

Saturday, September 4, 1943. We did our D.I.'s this morning and there aren't any "OPS." again tonite but we did night fighter affiliation—about a two hour flip. We were supposed to get mock Beaufighter attacks, but we didn't see any fighters during the whole flip. I have just eaten and am going to bed.

Sunday, September 5, 1943. After we did our D.I. today we were told we were on "OPS." tonite. We have a lot of gas so it looks like it is going to be a fairly long trip. We were supposed to be going to Munich, but it has been changed and we don't know what the new target is. We are taking off at 9 P.M. Briefing is at six o'clock so we are eating first, then going straight out to the kite.

Monday, September 6, 1943. Last nite we went to Mannheim—about a seven hour trip. It sure was a hot target—bags of searchlights and we could see fighters shooting our boys down away above us. We stooged in and when I pressed the bombing tit the bombs would go. Just then we were coned.* I called to George to jettison. Taffy saw a fighter coming on us. Normie did some wild evasive action. We finally got out of the searchlights at 3000 ft., but we lost the Pilot's escape hatch. It tore off the astro dome as it left. We flew all the way back with a terrific draught whipping thru the plane. We nearly froze, but we're back.

Tuesday, September 7, 1943. We got up early today and we hung around

* To be "coned" was to be caught in a searchlight from the ground.

150

waiting to hear if there were "OPS." on. There weren't any, so we got our leave passes and got paid, then George, Bill, Ray and I caught the six o'clock train to London. We arrived at Liverpool station at nine. Then Ray went to an Officers' hotel and we three checked in at the Albian Court Hotel. Newt doesn't seem to be here yet. We have just eaten in the canteen and then to bed.

Wednesday, September 8, 1943. Bill, George and I got up for breakfast and we ran into Newton in the dining room. I introduced the boys, then we went down town and met Ray Eberle. Then the five of us met Ray and had lunch, then Ray had a date so we four met "Jackie" (Newt's fiancee) and took her to the show.

Thursday, September 9, 1943. Newt and I got up for breakfast this morning, then we went downtown and met Jackie and a friend for lunch. Then Newt and I went to the photographer's to cancel former arrangements he made, as Jackie had her own. Then we went to the Victoria Hospitality League. Newt made arrangements for his honeymoon in Cambridge. Bed early tonite.

Friday, September 10, 1943. Newt and I got up for breakfast this morning and then I went downtown for lunch. While Newt went for the marriage license I went to see "Coney Island" this afternoon—not bad. Then I picked up the wedding dress and met Newt for dinner. Went to the Beaver Club then back to bed. George and Bill arrived back from Edinburgh.

Saturday, September 11, 1943. We all got up early this morning and went to the cleaner's and had our uniforms pressed. Normie arrived about 10. He, Bill and George gave Newt a pound as a wedding present. We went by tube and bus to Finchley, arriving just five minutes early. The wedding went off beautifully. Jackie looked lovely. I paid the minister and organist, then to Jackie's for the reception. Read telegrams to the bunch.

Sunday, September 12, 1943. I got up at 9:30—too late for breakfast—packed my stuff and took the tube to Waterloo. I arrived there at 11 to find about 300 people quequed[sic] up for the 11:30 train. I joined the queque[sic] and finally got in the train—had to stand all the way. Arrived in Bournemouth about 2:30.

Wednesday, September 15, 1943. We took off to do fighter affiliation today but just after we got off a kite pranged on the runway and our exercise was cancelled. We were told to land at Marren. We did on a grass field. It is a Mosquito Drome and we had a good look at them. They sure are nice jobs. All their crew went through our plane as it was quite a novelty to them. We ate there, took off and got back at 4 to be told we are on "OPS." tonite. What a rush!

Thursday, September 16, 1943. Last nite we went to the Dunlop rubber factory at Montluçon in Southern France. It was a piece of cake. We didn't see any flak, searchlights or fighters over the target. Black, oily smoke was rising to about 12,000 ft. We bombed from 5,500. Damn nearly got hit by flak coming back over the coast.

Friday, September 17, 1943. Last nite we went to Modane (8 hours) which is the only pass from France into Italy. We sure bombed the devil out of it. It was another piece of cake. No searchlights, flak or night fighters. It is right in the Alps and we flew over glaciers. Big party in the mess tonite.

Saturday, September 18, 1943. We have a stand down tonite. I doubt if anybody could have done "OPS." anyway as just about everybody had a hangover from last nite's mess party. The boys have all gone to Downham Market so I have peace and quiet to write my letters.

Sunday, September 19, 1943. We have the nite off again and I am going to bed good and early. I wonder why I always feel extra homesick on Sunday nites. All we did today was do our D.I. on the kite. Our ground crew are really nice chaps. They got us tea and cakes at 11 today.

Monday, September 20, 1943. Another night off and tonite Billy the Baker and I are going to Wisbech to see the sights. It is about fifteen miles from here and is about the size of King's Lynn which is about the same distance. We did formation flying and air-to-sea firing today.

Tuesday, September 21, 1943. We were scheduled for "OPS." tonite and just as we had done an extra good check on "ARF" the OP was cancelled, I think because of icing conditions. Bill and I went to the show in Wisbech. It isn't a bad town, rather old and has the buildings right up to the sidewalk which is only wide enough for one. We slept at a hostel and got the 6:45 bus back.

LETTER 82.

Daisey King
Maythorn
12 Western Road
Henley-on-Thames
Oxon., England
November 26th, 1943

My dear Agnes & Will,

I am just writing to thank you for your kind letter, & to say how truly sorry we are for you in your great loss. One can't realize it. To think we met & loved him & looked forward to his coming to see us. To be snatched away like that ... But there it was to be & it is lovely to think we had such a good time & we loved him like our own & he was so pleased to come & see us & last Xmas was really a jolly good time. The memory we shall never forget. Poor Uncle George was so proud of him & it has just about broken him up. He said he had never taken to anyone like he did George & he will never forget how he called him "Dad" as he was so much like his Dad.

George said don't write to you for a week or two to see if he received the parcel, but as nothing has come yet I thought I would write or you would not get it by Xmas. George received your letter—also Sally—& did you get the first one George wrote? Sally is fairly well. They have had such a lot of scares with the raids & yet they won't come down to Henley. I wrote & ask[ed] them in the beginning to give up there[sic] home & come down [and] I would manage them but, no, & it is just the same now. They are game to stick it out. Kathleen went to see them a little while ago & we both went in Sept., but I don't like travelling these dark days.

Well dear Agnes & Will, I shall have to close up. You have our deepest sympathy & hope perhaps if it is God's will he will turn up again one day. Don't give up faith & trust. Lots of love to you all from us all & will let you know if anything turns up.

From yours lovingly,
D.E. King

LETTER 83.

R155671
LAC MCCOWAN L.
R.C.A.F OVERSEAS
December 14th, 1943

Dear Aunt Agnes & Uncle Will,

Just a line to wish you both and also Bill a Merry Xmas and a happy New Year. I was very sorry to hear about George, and to offer condolences is rather futile so I'll just say, in closing, that I hope this war will be over soon.

Very best wishes,
Les.

LETTER 84.

L60771
GM. MCFARLANE R.H.
65TH A/TK BTY. R.C.A.
5TH CDN. A/TK. REGT.
CANADIAN ARMY
OVERSEAS
December 23rd, 1943

Dear Mrs. King & family,

It is with the very deepest regret that I have just heard that George will never come back. I heard a while ago that he was missing and I had been praying that he had come through it alright and was only a prisoner.

I don't know just what to say, Mrs. King. Mere words seem so useless. It seems so hard to believe that such a swell fellow can be gone. It was a terrible shock to me when Jim* went and now that George has gone too, it makes it all seem so terrible. I only hope that I have the chance soon to pay them back, and I think we will before very long.

There is one thing anyway, Mrs. King. He gave his life for a great cause, and you can be very proud of him. These boys must be very brave going over there at night. It certainly is no picnic.

And now Mrs. King, my very deepest sympathy to you all. It really has been a great loss.

Yours very sincerely,
Bob.

* Here, "Jim" refers to George's cousin James McCowan.

155

LETTER 85.

H. Edwards
Air Marshal
Headquarters of the Air Officer
Commanding-in-Chief
R.C.A.F. Overseas
Christmas, 1943

Dear Mr. King,

On this great day, in the lives of all good people, I would like you to know that I have not forgotten.

Sincerely,
H. Edwards, Air Marshal

LETTER 86.

George King
50 Mount View
Henley-on-Thames
Oxon., England
January 17, 1944

Dear Bill and Agnes,

I have just received your letter dated Nov. 28 and was pleased to hear from you. I should have written before but have been waiting to see if those parcles[sic] turned up. I am sorry Sally and Dais will not get their hose.

I was up at Daisy's the other day and am sorry to say she is not very well, but better than she has been. Will be up there again as soon as the weather gets better. We have had some terrible winds and fog and I can't get about like I used to do.

I had heard about poor old George. I sort of miss his coming to see me. We had some jolly times together. Last time he came he brought Billy Baker with him just for a few hours. Quite a nice young chap—sorry to hear he has got smashed up. I did not know any of the others, but George used to talk a lot about Spencer—his pilot, I think. How he used to say how much I talked like his dad. Thanks very much for the cutting from the paper. It is a good photo of him.

I am pleased to say I am keeping fairly well but the winter is very trying. Never two days alike but we are looking for better times in more senses than one. I hope you are both keeping well and all the family. With the best of love to all.

> From your loving brother,
> George

P.S. Best love from Dais and Tom.

LETTER 87.

Mrs. E. Morement
40 Trower Street
Frenchwood
Preston
Lancashire, England
January 20th, 1944

Dear Mrs King,

I feel I must express our deepest sympathy at the sad news you have by now doubtless received. We heard from the W.O.'s wife* and now again from Germany by our son on a postcard stating he has come out of hospital and expects W. Baker out soon. He gives no details or anything of their injuries. Four Canadian lads and one

---

* This refers to Mrs H. Hicks, the wife of Harold "Taffy" Hicks, the wireless operator in George's crew.

Welsh lad lost their lives and only by the grace of God two are left prisoners and alive. I hardly know how to write—it is a most difficult thing to express on paper how we feel about it. The wireless operator's mother we feel deeply shocked over. This is the third son she has lost and two more are at the same job but away from England. My husband's home is in the south, London in fact, and we are not far from Liverpool. My husband knows the Thames valley well. Churchill's prophesy[sic] certainly is really coming true.

Yours very sincerely,
E. Morement.

LETTER 88.

No 218 (Gold Coast) Squadron
Royal Air Force
Downham Market
Norfolk, England

Dear Mrs King,

I am in receipt of your letter dated 27th November 1943.

On behalf of the Squadron I would like to thank you for your kind offer that the shoes should be sold and the money placed to 218 (Gold Coast) Squadron Comforts Fund.

You will no doubt be interested to hear that the fund has benefited to the extent of 35/-.

Yours Sincerly[sic],
[signature illegible] F/L
for I.R. Ryall, Squadron Leader, Commanding
No 218 (Gold Coast) Squadron

LETTER 89.

Nessie Baker
121 Melville Avenue
Toronto, Ontario
February 7th, 1944

Dear Mrs. King,

No doubt you are thinking I had forgotten to write to you, but I have had trouble with my eyes. The specialist tells me when I got the word about Bill I had a shock & it has affected my eyes. Of coarse[sic] I wore glasses anyway & I suppose them being week[sic] has made them worse. But however I am getting to use the new glasses a little better. So I felt the first thing I would do was to write to you, dear.

I was sorry your brother did not come back to see us as we had no talk to him at all but maybe if he comes to Toronto again he could visit us. Well my dear I would like to tell you we had another card from Bill but no information—just that he was well & not to worry as the Red Cross was so good to him. So this made us feel a little happier. I think from what I can hear Mrs. Whylie[sic] and Mrs. Eberly[sic] had the same message as [you] which I don't think, Mrs. King, very definite.

I still feel that we are going to hear from the boys, so I do hope you are not giving up hope as we are still hoping & praying for that day to come when we are going to hear from them.

I have had no news from the boy's mother overseas,* yet I have written to them, so I expect I will be hearing. I do wish this terrible war was over & also that when it is we will all be able to meet each other & should it be that Bill is the only one to come home, I know

* Mrs Hicks was the mother of Harold Hicks, the wireless operator in George's crew. Harold's family in Cardiff, Wales, had just received word that he, too, had been killed.

159

he will want to meet all the mothers of his pals. Hoping to hear from you very soon. I remain

> Your true friend,
> Nessie Baker

LETTER 90.

> Mrs. H. Hicks
> 128 Rymney St.
> Cathay S.
> Cardiff
> S. Wales
> February 9th, 1944

Dear Mr. King,

I am indeed sorry that I have not written to you before but I mislaid the paper with the addresses of the boys but I am glad I have found it so I am writing to you and Mrs. Baker. Let me first say how sorry we are & we offer you our heartfelt sympathy in the loss of your dear son. My husband also gave his life with Sgt. Wylie, Pilot Spencer, [and] P.O. Eberle. Sgt. Baker & Sgt. Morement did everything they possibly could to save the others but with no avail—what heroes.

We were out in the garden the night that they went over as we heard them going our way & we prayed for their safe return, but little did we think that our dear boys were amongst them & that in less than 24 hrs we were to receive a telegram with the bad news. As we had the news on the 23rd Sept. at 4-30 it was a terrible shock, & a very bad shock for my husband's mother as she has lost 3 sons on air operations in 2 1/2 years. So you can understand what it meant to her & [her] family. My husband was home on leave 8 days before & he said what a fine bunch of boys they were & a jolly crowd. He was always talking about them & laughing & by what he used to tell us they must have been happy. We have a few nice snaps of them & your son is amongst them. They were taken a few weeks before they were lost & we were lucky to have them. I hope you had one. Sgt. Wylie & your son are standing & my husband & Sgt. Baker are kneeling—also Pilot Spencer is standing.

I have a baby 2 yrs old (Raymond) & Harold thought the world of him & he was a really good husband. My husband was 23 last month. He has 2 brothers left. The eldest is in India & the youngest is in Italy & one sister. We understand how you feel—we know it has upset us. The boys were always talking to my husband about their homes in Canada.

Mrs. Morement has had a few letters from her son so we hope that Mrs. Baker has also & that he is recovering from his wounds & may God keep them both safe & hope that they will be treated properly. So now dear Mr King I will close hoping to hear from you as you may have heard something about Sgt. Baker out there. So I will say good night & God bless you in your deep sorrow.

Sincerely,
Mrs. H. Hicks

LETTER 91.

Sallie King
55 Shirlock Road
Hampstead N.W.
London, England
February 16th, 1944

My dear Agnes & Will,

I got your letter a few days ago—what a long time they are coming. I was very pleased to get it, but the news is very sad. I can't say how one feels these days. Everybody seems to be so lonely, but as you say, perhaps it's all for the best that the dear boy is taken. You do know that there will be no more pain to bear. We must leave it all in God's hands. He knows best. It is all sorrow in these days. You will be sorry to hear poor Lottie is in hospital. Been there 11 weeks now. She had a stroke, & her mind is quite a blank. She knows us & is cheerful, but no memory—it's gone back to childhood. Oh dear, it's all so lonely & then to make matters worse I had a heart attack & fell down & fractured my wrist in two places. I have had it in plaster of Paris nearly 4 weeks now. I have to have another X-Ray next Tuesday, Shrove Tuesday. A good thing it's the left arm.

I am expecting Kathleen next Sunday. I hope she will be able to come—the travelling is so bad, & we have had a raid 4 nights running.

Please give my love to Jennie. I hope she is well & Bruce. I have not had her promised letter yet, & I hope Bill & Jim are well. How you must miss your baby boy. How disappointed I was not to see him again. He was having 7 days leave soon & coming to see me, & now it's all over. Poor Uncle George was very upset, & he is not at all well. Daisy says he can't get up to see them so often [with] this weather.

Now my dears, I must close. Not a very cheerful letter, but I know you will understand the lonelyness[sic]. With fondest love hoping you will keep well, & thanks for the cutting—it's nice to know how he was loved.

From your loving Sister,
Sallie

LETTER 92.

73-77 Oxford St.
London W.1.
April 4, 1944

Mr. G. King,
50 Mount View
Henley-on-Thames,
Oxford

Dear Mr. King,

It is with deep regret that I must confirm my telegram of November 12, 1943, regarding the death of your nephew, Sergeant George McCowan King.

There has been no further information received, other than that conveyed to you in my above mentioned telegram, however, I shall inform you immediately should any further news come to hand.

In view of the evidence received, and the lapse of time, action has accordingly been taken, to presume, for official purposes, that he lost his life on the 22nd September, 1943.

Please accept my profound sympathy in the loss of your nephew.

Yours sincerely,

R.K. Mann
    for A.B. Matthews, Wing Commander,
    for Air Officer Commanding-in-Chief,
    Royal Canadian Air Force, Overseas.

LETTER 93.

Robert Leckie
Air Marshal
Office of the Chief of the Air Staff
Ottawa, Ontario
April 11th, 1944

Dear Mr. King,

I have learned with deep regret that your son, Flight Sergeant George McCowan King, is now for official purposes presumed to have died on Active Service Overseas on September 22nd, 1943. I wish to offer you and the members of your family my sincere and heartfelt sympathy.

It is most lamentable that a promising career should be thus terminated and I would like you to know that his loss is greatly deplored by all those with whom your son was serving.

Yours sincerely,
    Robert Leckie
    Air Marshal, Chief of the Air Staff

LETTER 94.

J.G. Sparling, Squadron Leader
Command Chaplain (P)
No. 4 Training Command
Calgary, Alberta
April 14th, 1944

Dear Mr. King,

It is with deep regret that word has been received at this Headquarters that your son, Flight Sergeant George McCowan King, who was reported missing on the 22nd September, 1943, is now presumed, for official purposes, to have lost his life at that time.

You have been through an anxious time of waiting, hoping against hope that some good news would be forthcoming but apparently no word has been received. We owe a great deal of gratitude to our young men who have so willingly gone out to face danger and even make the supreme sacrifice in order that decency and justice may be preserved in the world. Our Christian faith at these times is a great help and our only comfort and may God give you courage and strength to bravely carry on.

Yours in sincerest sympathy,
J.G. Sparling, Squadron Leader
Command Chaplain

LETTER 95.

Sallie King
55 Shirlock Road
Hampstead N.W.
London, England
May 14, 1944

My dear Agnes & Will,

I have an idea I didn't write to say I had received the parcel. I know I acknowledged the dear boy's photo which stands just by the side of me, looking so natural at me. Well, I must thank you for all the good things you sent me. The prunes were quite nice altho' it was a month on the sea, & I liked all of it, especially the cheese spread. We don't see that here, at least I haven't come across it, but I don't go far shopping these days.

We are having some quiet nights just now. How I wish it was for good. I hope you are all well & that I shall hear from you soon. Lottie still keeps about the same—looks quite bright, but doesn't remember anything. It seems so sad to see her lying there & can't do anything for her.

I had Daisy & Kathleen up to see me on Easter Monday for a few hours. Dais was better but she has got so thin & she says George isn't at all well.

A friend of ours asked me over to her place for a week & I went & had a lovely change & rest. Wasn't it kind of them? It is so lonely on my own, but I mustn't grumble. My wrist has got better—a bit painful at times.

Love to you all. Hoping to hear from you soon. It's nice to get a cheery letter from you.

      With fondest love, from your loving sister,
        Sallie.

LETTER 96.

R155809
LAC KING J.
C.A.P.O. #4.
R.C.A.F. OVERSEAS.
NFLD.
June 1st, 1944

Dear Mother,

I haven't had any word from you for almost 2 weeks. The last I got was Dad's letter, so I've been wondering what's the matter, or maybe the letter went astray. I've been getting the News and Sun* quite regular—the News came today. I see Sask. is getting ready for a big election. Is old "Beef"† in good form? We had our half day off again today, but I didn't even play ball, but figure on going to the picture show tonight—Deanna Durbin in "The Amazing Mrs. Holliday." It's a real good show. I'm enclosing a money order for $40 for you to bank for me when you get the chance. I've saved all that since I came up here, and have quite a bit in me yet, so you can figure there isn't much to spend it on here. However, it will come in handy later on.

Stevie‡ and some of the boys have been getting innoculations[sic], etc., but I'm right up to date in mine, so don't have to take any just now. My system should be pretty full of serum anyway. Some of the guys were out fishing again Sun. and caught some real nice ones, but I had to work for a while Sun.

I saw in one of the papers that "Buck" Fisher of Wadena was now reported safe in the U. Kingdom—he'd been missing quite a while too, hadn't he?

We haven't been very busy lately. I'm still doing engine work, but

* Jim's family had been sending him copies of the Wolseley News, as well as copies of the Grenfell Sun.

† "Beef" Dundas was a Saskatchewan Liberal M.L.A. from the Summerberry district.

‡ "Stevie" refers to a serviceman named Stevenson, from Mortlach, Saskatchewan.

167

with pay parades, clothing parades, going down to get my boots repaired, etc., I haven't been in the hangar an awful lot for the last week. Ed Holkestead* gets the Leader all the time so I see it quite a bit. He's been here since last Aug. and is going on leave sometime this month. I sure wouldn't mind going out with him—his home's near Mossbank.

Rolie† chipped the bone in his thumb playing softball last Sat. afternoon, so it's been pretty sore, but he was playing again today. So apparently it wasn't a very big chip. We had quite a game Sat. and Sun. night we went for quite a hike, but that's about the extent of our activities. When I'm not working I stick pretty close to my old bunk.

I suppose the crops are all in out there now. I've heard reports of rain in Sask., so hope you got your share. It's always so much nicer when things are green.

There sure isn't anything to write about, and not having heard from you for so long makes it even worse, as I can't even comment on things in the district.

There aren't nearly as many Westerners here as there were at Scoudouc, and a lot more from Ontario. I always get along a lot better with the Westerners and Maritimers—they don't think they're so clever for the most part. You'd never run into a better bunch of guys than we had at Scoudouc. I see Stu Crawford‡ is discharged (honorably) from the Air Force—was it because his father wasn't well?

This seems to be all for now. Hoping to hear from you soon, and also that the money order gets there O.K. I may be crazy, but I don't like mailing my letters open.§ I'll sure hang on to my receipt till I hear you got it alright.

The cold I had got better pretty quick, and I escaped without getting a cough like usually follows a cold.

* Ed Holkestead was a serviceman from Mossbank, Saskatchewan.

† Keith Roland was a serviceman from Beamsville, Ontario.

‡ Stu Crawford was a serviceman from the Summerberry district.

§ Officers, as gentlemen who presumably could be trusted, were not required to submit their letters to military censors, although their correspondence could be monitored on occasion. Enlisted men, on the other hand, were required to submit each letter, unsealed, to a military censor, who checked its content before mailing it. While in theory all enlisted men's mail was censored, the sheer volume of mail meant that in practice this did not always happen.

Your loving son,
Jim.

P.S. I just heard over the radio that there was no show tonight, so I guess that's my night's entertainment shot. I'll have to find something else to amuse myself. J.K.

LETTER 97.

Royal Canadian Air Force
Estates Branch
Ottawa, Ontario,
June 8, 1944

Mr. William King,
Summerberry, Saskatchewan
Re: KING, George McCowan F/S (Deceased)
No. R142247 R.C.A.F.

Dear Mr. King:

Thank you for the completion and return of our Form P.64.

It is advised that we have on file your son's will dated the 17th of December, 1941, wherein you are named the sole beneficiary and appointed sole executor of his estate. If a later will is discovered Overseas you will be so advised.

Yours very truly,
Director of Estates.

LETTER 98.

Summerberry, Sask.
June 18, 1944

The Secretary
Department of National Defence for Air
Ottawa, Canada

Dear Sir:

My son, Flt. Sgt. Geroge McCowan King, R142247, R.C.A.F., was reported killed on Sept. 22nd, 1943 by the International Red Cross at Geneva. The raid was over Hanover. I have not been notified as to the location of his grave. If you have any information regarding it, would you please notify me?

Yours sincerely,
William King.

LETTER 99.

L60771
GM. McFarlane R.H.
65th Bt. R.C.A.
5th Cdn. A/TK Regt.
Canadian Army Overseas
June 20th, 1944

Dear James,

Was very pleased to hear from you again. I was beginning to wonder how you were getting on, and what part of the country you were in at present. I don't imagine Newfoundland is any great place to be stuck, though. There can't be a heck of a lot to do out there.

Are there any cities or towns around that you can go to if you get a leave?

Yes, I guess we will have a few good parties back there, when all the fellows get back, although as you say, there will be a lot of the fellows missing, and it will seem strange not having them around. Somehow it's hard to believe, though, that George and Jim have gone, though. Especially George—it only seems a short while ago that we were having such a swell time for that month that I stayed up with you.

Well, things have finally got started over here now, so pretty well all the boys will soon be in action either in Italy or here. Quite a few went into France at the start, and seemed to give a very good account of themselves. Hope it isn't long before we are there.

The Germans have been sending over a lot of these pilotless planes of theirs the past few days, but I don't think they will amount to much. We've seen the fighter planes shooting them down here. Saw them shoot down quite a few last night just like clay pidgeons[sic]—a burst or two of machine gun fire, and they'd dive to the ground and explode.

Thanks for all the good wishes, James. Hope to be able to return them someday soon. I've been married for over 3 months now, but we've only been able to be together for about 2 weeks, as the wife works in Glasgow. She had a week's holidays a little while ago, so came and stayed down here. I was quite suprised[sic], though, when I heard Doug was getting married too. His wife has left the Air Force now, and they live in Davidson. He seems to think it's alright, although I guess he can't run around all over the country with the ball teams like he used to. His wife used to be quite a ball player, too—she used to pitch a lot in the northern Sask. league, and she was pretty good at most other sports.

There can't be a heck of a lot of the girls left around S.berry now that were there that winter I was up. I guess most of them will have gone to the cities and got jobs other places.

I guess they have had quite a lot of rain back home again this spring, so crops should be pretty good again. They are pretty busy at home just now building a new house. It is a pretty big one, and they are building it out of a lot of this new building material, so it should be pretty nice when it is finished. George* has quit school now, and he does most of the work on the land with the tractor.

Well, I guess we've got something new back in Sask. now with the C.C.F. in power now. Well, they've been trying long enough, so I guess they will be pretty happy now. I guess we'll just have to wait and see now if they will do half of all the wonderful things they used to promise, or if they will be about the same as all other political parties and their promises.

Well, that seems to be about all for now, James. Thanks again for writing and remember, I'm always glad to hear from any of the old gang. Please give the folks at home my best wishes.

>Your old pal,
>Bob.

* George was Bob and Doug McFarlane's younger brother.

LETTER 100.

Daisey King
Maythorn
12 Western Road
Henley-on-Thames
Oxon., England
June 22nd, 1944

My dear Agnes & Will,

At last I have received the parcel you so kindly sent. Quite in good order it arrived 16 June—about 3 months coming, yet Sallie had hers quite a month ago. Still we are very lucky to get it at all these days, & thank you very much.

I put the prunes straight into soak & we had them on Sunday with a custard. The sultanas—what fine ones—I put in a cake. Cheese was just what we wanted. We only get 3d* worth a week & Tom likes to take it for his nightly watching. So you may guess we are not so piggy with it, & he is watching five nights weekly. The soap too is very acceptable—we have to give points too[sic] soap, like most things. I see we are going to get figs, dates, & prunes on the market, but really we don't do too bad. We have a lot to be thankful for.

Sallie is not at all well—her leg is bad. I do wish she would lock up her home & come down for a time till they have finished sending those pilotless planes over—beastly things, they are. Lottie is not better & is quite senile—don't even know Sallie only for a minute. That is what makes it so bad for Sallie because half the home is hers. If she was gone she would know what to do. Kay† & I went up to see her Whit Monday but I don't care about going to London these days. George is a lot better but not too grand but he has got his time and

* "3d" means "3 pence."

† "Kay" refers to Kathleen, who was Daisey's daughter.

173

wages altered. He goes to work every week 4 days a week & more money instead of fortnightly so now he goes to the British Resturant[sic] for his dinner every day & he feels better for his extra food. They have a good dinner for a 1/- meat & veg. pudding & a cup of tea,* no cooking or washing up for you, as his rashions[sic] were very small for one person. I generally go on Friday. It makes a nice change & our larder is very nearly empty by then. Tom cooks himself an egg & chip potatoes. He dosen't[sic] go to the resturant[sic] as he coughs so much, everybody turns round & looks at him. He can't even go to the Cinema just now. It is a worry for him & me too. We are not having very nice weather—so cold & a lot of wind & no rain.

How are you & Will feeling now? Hope W[ill's] rhumatism[sic] is better & you are getting over your trouble a bit. Time helps to heal the wound. I have the dear boy's photo standing on my table and talk to him. It is a lovely one of him.

How are the other boys getting on? You don't want them to get to England to get such bad treatment. Hope Jenny is well & still busy I expect. We shall be so thankful when this war is over. We are having a busy week for "Salute the Soldiers."† Something on every day. They hope to realize 300,000 pounds, & I expect they will get it. Kathleen is very well. She comes home every Sunday for a few hrs. I look forward to her coming. She comes at 1/4 to 2 & goes back at 4-15. I generally go up to see her off by bus at the Town Hall, & it is crowded. Phil & his wife are very well, but worked to death, & in the thick of every thing, & they get so tired. They work so many hrs, especially Phil, & don't get home very often.

I am feeling a bit better now but soon get tired & don't want to work like I used to. Have not got my sister here now. She wanted too much waiting on & I did not feel like waiting on her, a great big fat

* "1/-" stands for "1 shilling," or 12 pence.

† "Salute the Soldiers" was a military fundraising campaign.

174

thing, so it is nice to be alone.

Well my dears I must draw to a close & write 2 more letters. My very many thanks to you both & the best of love & good wishes from us all at Henley.

From your affectionate sister,
Dais & Tom & George

P.S. I forgot to say thanks for the stockings. They will be lovely for next winter & I like the colour. Thanks very much.

LETTER 101.

R155809
LAC KING J.
C.A.P.O. #4.
R.C.A.F. OVERSEAS.
NFLD.
July 5th, 1944

Dear Mother,

Just a few lines to let you know I'm still knocking around. I received your welcome letter Sun., and was glad to hear you were all in good health, and getting along pretty well. You needn't have worried about not putting your name on the parcel, as I wouldn't have mistaken that shortbread anywhere. Everything was sure swell. It's all gone now but the quart of chicken—we're saving that for a picnic some day when the 4 of us can go out together. Fred and I seem to be getting lots of time off, but they keep poor Rolie and Steve on the jump. Fred and I had our 3 days' leave, then got loaned to another section that have a system where each man gets a 5 day pass a month, and after working for 5 days there we were called in and given our 5 days for the month of July. That's pretty good isn't it—8 days off in 2 wks. We were going to Grand Falls, but think we'll wait till next month, and then maybe the other fellows will be able to come too. So we're going to spend it loafing, canoeing, swimming, etc. You asked who Fred is. I told you when we got posted, I think. His name is Fred Wiese, from Innisfail, Alta. Rolie is Keith Roland, of Beamsville, Ont., and of course Stevenson is from Mortlach. We'd all been in the same section at Scoudouc, and known one another for over a year. Fred is a quiet fellow. He worked on the exp. farm at Strathmore, Alta., before joining up. Rolie is more the rowdy type, always on the go, and Stevie—he's a typical little farmer. We have lots of fun together, and stay together most of the time. They always have Fred and I working together. He doesn't always approve of my methods. He's a guy who has to do everything exactly on schedule.

The pyjamas haven't arrived yet. It was too bad I put you to all the trouble. I don't think I'll sell any, as they may be hard to get for a while. I'll let you know when I need the shorts. I'll send the money probably after next payday, as I'll be sending some for you to bank then. You seem to be smarter than a lot, as some of the fellows' parents couldn't manage to get them any.

The cold I had turned into a cough, and I've coughed quite a bit these last few days. It's almost too hot to think in here. The last few nights it's been pretty hard to get to sleep for the heat.

What made Kerrs* decide to settle down in Wolseley? I would have thought they would have gone down around Carlyle. What's the new minister like, or is he there yet? Our ball team has taken a couple of bad beatings lately, so we're not near the top of the league anymore. So you sold old Chips—she was a wonderful old cow. I hope she's left

* The Kerrs—Patsy's family—were the family of the United Church minister at Summerberry. They moved to Wolseley in 1944.

a good heifer. That wasn't too bad a price you got—she wasn't near as big as Min or Daisy, nor as fat. Of course, the fellow wouldn't pay any more than he could get away with.

I don't imagine Crossmans would thank Mrs. J.B. for telling that Verna was adopted. In fact, they didn't tell me. One day when Mr. Crossman and Orma were at school Mrs. Crossman asked me who I thought the girls looked like. I said Orma looked like Stanley Bowering, but couldn't say who Verna looked like, so apparently they don't want it spread around. Verna is an awful cute little kid.

Is Bill taking in any of the dances or sports days that they always have around this time of year? Had I stayed at Scoudouc I would have tried to get home for those two weeks. However, I have 3 mos. in here. In another 3 I'll be able to get furlough and 7 days' isolation leave, and a new order has come out giving you travelling time both ways. That will leave me 21 days at home if it isn't changed before then. So maybe I'll be able to spend a couple of days with Jennie and Bruce. She's after me again to promise to go up. Maybe you or Dad could come with me. The time here goes fairly fast, so it won't be long till I'm home again. The show is out, so I won't have much more peace to write once Rolie arrives. I was to a show Sun., "The Case of Dr. Wassel," and didn't care for it. The one tonight is "Cobra Woman." One good thing—we get the very latest shows here, before they're released in Canada even.*

Well this seems to be all for now, so I'll say so long for now.

Your loving son,
Jim.

---

* In 1944, Newfoundland was not yet part of Canada and was considered to be "overseas."

LETTER 102.

Ottawa, Canada
July 11th, 1944

Mr. William King,
Summerberry, Saskatchewan.

Dear Mr. King:

In reply to your letter of June 18th, regarding your son, Flight Sergeant George McCowan King, I am indeed sorry that in spite of every effort made by the International Red Cross Society at Geneva, they have been unable to obtain the location of your son's grave.

I feel sure you will understand that due to conditions as they exist in Europe, it is not always possible to obtain this information, and in many other instances, it is obtainable only after very many months.

I do wish to assure you, however, that the International Red Cross Society is continuing its enquiries and any word received will be forwarded to you at once.

May I again offer you my deepest sympathy.

Yours sincerely,
[signature illegible]
R.C.A.F. Casualty Officer,
for Chief of the Air Staff.

LETTER 103.

Daisey King
Maythorn
12 Western Road
Henley-on-Thames
Oxon., England
July 23, 1944

My dear Will and Agnes,

I thought I would write you a few lines to say I have at last got
Sallie down here, & am afraid it is too late. She came on the 5th July.
Phil went over & packed her a few things & took her to Paddington in
a car. I met her at Henley—that was a Wed. She managed to get to the
town on Thursday & Friday for her ration books exchanged, her
pension put through. On Sat she seemed worn out so I said, "Just you
stay in bed today dear." Well there she is now of course. I had the Dr.
He has been very good & said she is absolutely worn out & her heart is
in a dreadful state all over the place. She may get over it for a time—
then again she might go any time. You see those old doodle bugs were
so frightening there was no peace or rest. She could not even undress.
Then I wrote again, not the first time, & she said yes she would be
pleased to come, & her great worry as well was poor old Lottie. She is
still in hospital & now she is quite mental. Sallie has done everything
& paid for everything if anything happens to her. She can't do
anything else, so she just leaves her in God's hands. Now I will do all I
can for Sallie. She is so gentle & sweet & perhaps with the rest & quiet
nights we get she may get better. My hubby would be so [happy] to
know I was doing all I could for her. She talks a good deal about the
old days when they were all little. George is very concerned about her

& comes up each Monday but it takes it out of him. It is a long way from his home to mine. Of course Sally has not been up yet to see his little house.

You see, when the war started I asked Lottie & Sally to give up there[sic] home & come down to Henley but they said they would be alright. The did not think it would be such a dreadful time as we have had. Then for the last 2 yrs. she has had Lottie bad & now between it all it has nearly killed her, at her age, in her 83rd year.

We are not having very nice weather—it is so dull. Can't think where the sun has gone. Do hope this wretched war will soon be over. We are all tired of it. Hope all the boys are well, also Jennie. My love to you all. I have not told Sallie I am writing to you. Hope Will's rhumatism[sic] is better (old age creeping on). Now my dear Agnes I will close with much love to you all. I remain

> Your loving sister,
> Daisey King

P.S. I will write again soon if there is anything special to say. D.K.

LETTER 104.

R155809
LAC KING J.
C.A.P.O. #4.
R.C.A.F. OVERSEAS.
NFLD.
August 16th, 1944

Dear Mother,

I just got back from the country last night; and received your letter and wire. Thanks very much for remembering me.* I was out on the same kind of work that I used to do at Scoudouc, and it was sure funny—the natives there hadn't seen a stranger in their lives. We flew in by sea-plane, and back out. Wherever we went a whole tribe of kids followed us. The seemed to think we were miracle men. They certainly lead a humble life, and would give you anything.

Don't worry about not sending me a box, as I know how hard it is to get anything, and how busy you are at this time of year. The last time I wrote I forgot to mention the ring. I think that's a good idea, but don't know the size. One of my chum's rings fits me fine, but he doesn't know the size either.

So Bill started cutting? How is the crop, anyway? You've certainly sold a lot of cattle, and at a pretty good price, but you won't have any more to sell for a while now.

Barbara really disgraced herself, didn't she? I saw a cartoon the other day of a kid whose mother was apparently going to the beach, and they were in a street car, and the kid had stripped himself and got out his sand shovel. The mother was saying, "You may have waited till we got there." I would have sent it if I could locate it. I've always

* Jim's birthday was on 12 August.

answered Norma's and Jean's letters, so maybe one of them has gone astray. However, I wrote Norma just about a week ago, so she'll probably have it now. Jennie hasn't written for months, but maybe she will now that she's back from the holiday.

Dad really was barking up the wrong tree when he tried to get the low-down on the raspberries from the Heinnemans.* You're lucky you didn't get chased out too.

You say I'll soon be an old bachelor, and that I should start looking around. What do you expect a poor guy to do out in this country? Do you want me to bring home a "Newf?"

The meals here are picking up a bit. They had roast turkey for dinner yesterday, and we had mince pie for des[s]ert. They sure have some pretty bare meals. In this place that we were, 3 of us used to borrow a boat and row a couple of miles across the bay every night, so I can say that I've been on the ocean in a rowboat. I'm getting to be pretty fair at rowing and paddling, but there were 5 girls in a boat one night, and we were half way over when they started and they beat us over. And they were only about 15 years old.

There doesn't seem to be very much to say this time. That fortune teller really hit the nail on the head when he said Mrs. Orville Crozier† had a great worker for a husband. That should flatter old Orville.

I guess I'll have to close this up for now, as there really isn't anything to say.

Thurs. I left this open last night, and so thought I'd add a few lines today. The meals are sure picking up. We had cornflakes for breakfast and ice cream at dinner today. There's a good show on here tonight, Frank Sinatra in "Step Lively," so I think I'll go.

Two of the fellows who I was working with feel sort of sickly—a touch of the flu or something. I hope it misses me.

* Fred Heinneman farmed near Summerberry.

† Orville Crozier and his wife Luella farmed near the Kings.

I see by the news that I got tonight that Pete Hewitt's* was a $3000 fire. Also his card of thanks—I thought that was pretty good about a friend being a precious thing. Old Pete would have to get his little moral in.

Well, this seems to be all for now.

Your loving son,
Jim.

P.S. You can show the clipping to Norma & Jean if you see them. J.K.

LETTER 105.

R155809
LAC KING J.
C.A.P.O. #4.
R.C.A.F. OVERSEAS.
NFLD.
August 17th, 1944

Dear Mother,

Seeing one of the boys who live out that way is going on leave today, I thought I'd drop you a few lines to let you know what's what.† You can't say very much in ordinary letters, and this one will be posted at B'view‡ or along there somewhere. The unit I came up with—19 sub. repair depot—disbanded, and we were spread all over. Some of the boys went back to the Maritimes, but Fred, Steve and I are still here. I'm working in the servicing flight. We refuel and check all visiting planes, such as the transports between here and Can., the overseas mail planes, etc. That's the Lancaster you see the pictures of. I put 1492 gals. of gas in it the other day, and sent her on her way over. They have all the big planes here—Liberators, Fortresses, etc., and some of those mighty B-29's that bombed Japan were in here. They're really massive planes.

We came over on the Lady Rodney, sister ship of the Lady Nelson. You know—the hospital ship. I've seen it twice in Halifax. We had quite a little convoy, and landed at St. John's Nfld. Newfie is quite a wild country, all bush, rocks and swamp. This airport was built on a swamp. The weather isn't too bad, however, but there's quite a bit of fog. We had an awful fire here in June—a hangar, 4 Liberators, and a lot of equipment. A depth charge in one of the planes blew, and broke windows for half a mile.

Let me know if you get this O.K. Just say "I got your letter" or something like that. All the boys send out mail with the fellows going on leave.

There doesn't seem to be much else, but I just thought seeing I had the chance, I'd write a few lines and let you know what I was doing.

       Your loving son,
        Jim.

LETTER 106.

Chief of the Air Staff
Royal Canadian Air Force
Ottawa, Ontario
August 18th, 1944

Dear Mr. King,

R.142247 Sgt. King, G.M.

Enclosed herewith are the following original documents which were submitted by the above noted on enlistment in the Royal Canadian Air Force:

1 Birth Certificate
1 Grade Twelve Diploma
1 First Aid Certificate (St. John Ambulance Association)

Yours truly,
E. Stewart
for T.K. McDougall, Group Captain
for Chief of the Air Staff.

Encls.

LETTER 107.

R155809
LAC KING J.
C.A.P.O. #4.
R.C.A.F. OVERSEAS.
NFLD.
September 4th, 1944

Dear Mother,

I received your welcome letter some time last week, and was glad to hear you were all well. Too bad about the rain. So a plane was forced down there—that would cause a little excitement.

I inquired about my leave, and I guess I can get it sometime around the end of this month, which should be better. I'm not just sure when. You can never tell exactly when you'll get away, as it's hard to get out at times. They fly you as far as Moncton, so it won't take me any longer than it used to, and besides, I get 8 days' travelling time.

They're really working me hard these days—at least keeping me on the run. Another fellow and I were working on 3 different jobs at the same time. I should have a 48 sometime this week, so I'll get rested up then. The guy I'm working with was stationed at Davidson for over a year, and knew Doug McFarlane well. The thing that seemed to impress him most about Douglas was his laugh, so apparently he never outgrew that cackle. I owe Bob McFarlane a letter. I wrote him awhile ago, and he answered, but gosh knows where he may be now. The Br., Cans., and Yanks are really going to work in France and Belgium just now. The Germans don't seem to be putting up much resistance. They must be really beaten or have a surprise ready is my idea.

Fred isn't back from the bush yet, and Stevie left on his harvest leave, so I'm more or less alone as far as the old gang is concerned.

I took my old uniform down to the tailor and got it condemned. Now all I have to do is get it cleaned and then get a new one, so I ought to have a new uniform for my leave. I also wore out another pair of boots—at least they need new heels and soles.

I never got that gum that Jennie sent. She sent for it through the company, so it will likely take quite a long while to arrive, but will be welcome when it does come. There was a pretty good show here last night—"Thousands Cheer."

I saw in the Leader where Jeff Strudwick* got married in Regina, and "Speed" Yeast was the best man. I was supposed to have been at that wedding if I'd stayed at Scoudouc, as we were all 3 going home on leave together. I don't know whether Fred and I will be able to go out together or not.

We've been playing a lot of crib lately in the barracks. My luck seems to be pretty good. At least I win more than I lose.

So Bill Harries put a hammer through the cylinder of his combine? I can just hear him piping about that time.

Well, this seems to be all for just now, so I'll close for tonight. Maybe I'll write sooner next time, and let you know approximately when to expect me, but you often wait several days to get out. I'm certainly looking forward to seeing you again. It's just a few days better than a year since I left last year.

Your loving son,
Jim.

* Geoffrey Strudwick was a fellow serviceman of Jim's from Pilot Butte, who later settled in Regina.

LETTER 108.

Kathryn Spencer
114 Broughton
Montreal 28
Quebec
September 5th, 1944

Dear Mrs. King,

I sincerely hope this finds you well. I have been saving these snaps for you and so hope you will find them a comfort. That is the way they are to me.

I started out in June to spend my vacation with Mae Wylie and here I am still in Montreal. I miss home very much but the change is a very good thing.

The Wylies are a very nice family. I spent 3 weeks with them and it was lots of fun. There are 2 girls, 2 boys, Mae & Mrs Wylie.

Mrs. Wylie has been in pretty poor health but she's a truly grand person, and Mae & I get along very well.

Coming out we passed through Summerberry and I thought of you.

From Toronto I went on to New York to visit one of my big brothers. I was certainly impressed with the place and had two very sore feet and a stiff neck for a week after. From there I came to Montreal to stay with another big brother and decided to take a job and stay for a while—not for long. The winters I hear are bitterly cold and anyway I think there's no place like Vancouver anywhere. I thought the prairies were lovely. So I've come quite a long way and it's my first train trip.

I saw Mrs. Baker but she had nothing to say about Bill. I didn't go to see the Eberles because they have had a very hard time of it lately with sickness and I felt it would not be the best thing to do.

Mae came up to see me from Toronto last weekend and we had [a] very nice visit. She's a very sweet girl and I like her very much.

I guess this is your busy season on the prairie—or have you finished? My folks are from Regina and though they love the Coast they talk and talk about the prairies.

Mr. & Mrs. Spencer are in good health. I'm sure they would want me to send you their very kindest regards along with my own.

> Sincerely,
> Kathryn Spencer

LETTER 109.

> R155809
> LAC KING J.
> C.A.P.O. #4.
> R.C.A.F. OVERSEAS.
> NFLD.
> September 10th, 1944

Dear Bill,

It seems quite a while since I wrote to you so here goes for a few lines. You seem to be getting on well with the harvesting. Who do you figure on threshing with?

We had today off to attend the big sports meet. They sure had a fine day for it too, and the Air Force seemed to hold their own and a little better. I should have got in condition and participated, as the best hop-step-and-jump was 35' 6", and I did 34' 6" when I was 16 at one of the school sports [meets]. The pole vaulters went 10' 6" and the high jumpers 5' 4". I got a great kick out of the tug-o-war. You should have seen our Air Force team, all of them about my height and weighing a good 200 lbs—they pulled the poor army guys all over the field. Remember the day old Matt camped on the end of the women's rope that time at the old-timers' picnic? I always think of that when I see a tug-o-war.

Fred and I went to see "Claudia" at the Can. theatre tonight, and it was real good—an entirely different type of show to what you usually see, and Thurs., "This is the Army" is coming. I've seen it but it's real good.

My furlough is supposed to start on Oct. 2nd, so at that rate I'll be home around the 5th or 6th, which ought to be O.K. as mother said the 10th would be alright.

The people at home must have had a real field day when the plane took off from Uncle Jim's field. What did you think of it?

Thanks very much for renewing my sub. to the Sun. You keep me really stocked up with newspapers, and I always like to get them. I got all 3 yesterday.

I've been pretty busy of late, but don't seem to be suffering from overwork. However, it's a change to keep moving.

Fred and I will be able to travel out together, but his extra couple of days travelling time will make it a different day when we report back to Moncton. I may be at Moncton for a few days waiting transportation back, and if so will be able to look up some of my old chums at Scoudouc.

I don't think I told mother all the particulars of that dance I was at up in the backwoods. Well, there was a barrel of home-made beer sitting in the corner of the room, and an old tin pitcher beside it, so if anyone needed refreshments they just dipped out a jug. There was yeast, slices of potato etc. floating around in it. I never saw such a concoction in my life, and did I mention that in one square set there were two girls who looked just alike, and wore the same kind of dress? They were sisters, and just as I was getting on famously, I got into the same set as them, and one was my partner, and after we'd circle the room and then start to swing, I'd always catch the wrong one. It was a never-to-be-forgotten hoe-down.

We have quite a few good old crib games here at night. In fact, a lad named Watkin has challenged me for as soon as I finish this letter. He's still grumbling about last night. He needed 8 to go out and just had enough to do it, and first count. So we played 3 eights in a row, me having the first and last, the last one making 31 for eight points which put me out. It's a great way to pass the time.

How is "eem"* getting on? I haven't heard much of them lately. I can just see Bill Harries putting the hammer through his new combine.

Well, this seems to be about all for just now. Hoping to see you all in a little better than 3 weeks. I hope this finds yourself, Dad, and Mother all in good health. You were lucky to get young Les† to do some stooking.

      Your aff. bro.,
      Jim.

P.S. How is the ammunition situation? I hope there's enough to shoot a few chickens when I get out there. J.K.

* I am not sure who "eem" refers to, but it must have been a private joke about someone from the district, perhaps the Harrieses, as Bill Harries is mentioned two sentences later.

† George and Jim's cousin "young Les"—who had been serving in England—had been home to Summerberry and helped with the harvest.

191

LETTER 110.

Kathryn Spencer
114 Broughton
Montreal 28
Quebec
September 25th, 1944

Dear Mrs. King,

Thanks for your nice letter and for your kind invitation to come and see you. I would certainly love to meet you and would be just tickled pink to have a chance to see how you farm and the horses and all. That's something I've never seen and always wanted to.

I'm very sorry to hear you will be having an operation. I'll certainly be thinking about you and am sure it will be a complete success with Jeannie there to take care of you. It will be good for you to have James home before you have it—and won't he be thrilled to get home after being at Gander. I hear it's the lonliest[sic], coldest station in Canada. He'll probably eat you out of house and home.

On the other hand, I've got such a darn interesting job here I honestly hate to think of giving it up. Oh, how I wish it could be in Vancouver. So I'm going to stay at it at least another two months or maybe 3 if I can take the cold weather and go home in time for Christmas. That means I can't accept your invitation for October, but I do thank you very sincerely and hope it may be possible some time.

I haven't much praise for this part of the country compared to the West, but I was up to the Laurentian Mountains this week-end and they are truly lovely—soft and green and rolling and very picturesque indeed. French Canada is lots more French than anything else and lots of the aspects are anything but picturesque.

I hear from Mae Wylie regularly and they are all fine according to her. Doug's mother is a wonderful person. They thought your son was a very fine man.

Don't work too hard getting that good crop in, will you?

Sincerely,
K. Spencer

LETTER 111.

R155809
LAC KING J.
Fort William, Ontario.
October 22nd, 1944

Dear Mother,

Have had a good trip so far.* Saw Aunt Georgie. John and Les, two fellows I used to work with at Scoudouc, are on the train, and Fred was to Wpg., where he's stopping for a day. Hope you are all fine.

Love,
from Jim.

* Jim sent this brief postcard as he was on his way back to Newfoundland after he had spent his leave at home on the farm.

LETTER 112.

Estates Branch
Ottawa, Canada
October 25, 1944

Mr. William King,
Summerberry, Saskatchewan
Re: KING, George McCowan F/S (Deceased)
No. R142247 R.C.A.F.

Dear Mr. King,

    We wish to advise you that your son's personal effects which were located Overseas have now reached this Branch and will be forwarded to you within the next few days in a carton by prepaid express and a parcel by registered mail. We trust that they will reach you in good condition and would ask that upon their arrival you complete and return to this Branch the enclosed form of receipt.

       Yours faithfully,
          Director of Estates

Encl.

LETTER 113.

Estates Branch
Ottawa, Ontario,
February 19, 1945

Mr. William King,
Summerberry, Saskatchewan
Re: <u>KING, George McCowan F/S (Deceased)</u>
No. R142247 R.C.A.F.

Dear Mr. King:

Distribution can now be made of the monies held here at credit to the Service Estate of your late son.

The total available to this Branch for distribution is $121.22 – being made up as shown in the following statement:

Cash in Effects $14.51
Balance of Pay $106.71
Total $121.22

You are entitled to this money as the sole Beneficiary named in your son's Will.

Treasure has been requested to forward a cheque payable to your order in the above amount of $121.22 directly to you at an early date. Please complete and return to this Branch the enclosed receipt form after the cheque has reached you.

Yours faithfully,
L.M. Firth, Colonel
Director of Estates.

Encl.

LETTER 114.

R.C.A.F. Casualty Officer
For Chief of the Air Staff
Royal Canadian Air Force
Ottawa, Ontario
June 21st, 1945

Dear Mr. King,

Our Overseas Headquarters have forwarded to this Headquarters a statement made by Warrant Officer A.W. Baker, a member of the crew with your son, Flight Sergeant George McCowan King. Warrant Officer Baker was a Prisoner of War but has now been liberated.

He states that their aircraft crashed on September 22nd, 1943, just outside of Hanover, Germany, and he was told that your son and all members of the crew with the exception of himself and Sergeant Morman[sic], a Royal Air Force member of the crew, lost their lives. I realize that this information can be of little solace to you, but I felt you would wish to be informed of Warrant Officer Baker's statement.

There are several Services set up in [an] endeavour to find all particulars possible of crashed aircraft. Some information is available concerning a great many aircraft which crashed or were shot down by the enemy, and every possible effort on an organized basis is being put forth to secure all information available. It is the duty of the Graves Registration Units, which are under the control of the Military Authorities, to enquire for and locate the graves of all personnel known to [or] believed to have crashed and to have been buried in occupied areas.

A Royal Air Force and Dominion Air Force Missing Research and Enquiry Service has been organized for the purpose of research and enquiry in liberated territories into the circumstances of aircrews reported as casualties. This Service endeavours to obtain additional information to supplement that already received. The Civilian population of these areas is being contacted by Radio, Press, and Proclamations through the various civic authorities to centralize through this Service any information or concrete evidence they may have about Air Force personnel or crashed aircraft. Similar instructions have been issued to all Service personnel in these areas.

I wish to again assure you that when any additional information is received concerning your son it will be forwarded to you. However, I am sure you will realize that owing to the great chaotic conditions existing in Europe at the present time and the great number of enquiries confronting these enquiry Service[s], some time may pass before more information is received.

May I again offer you and the members of your family my deep sympathy in your great loss.

> Yours sincerely,
> [signature illegible]
> R.C.A.F. Casualty Officer,
> for Chief of the Air Staff

LETTER 115.

F/SGT W. MOREMENT
40 Trower Street
Frenchwood
Preston Lanes
Lancashire, England
June 23rd, 1945

Dear Mr & Mrs King,

I wish to thank you for the letters written to Mother. They have been very reassuring—she has looked forward to every one.

I met Bill Baker the morning after we came down & we had a good talk, but we couldn't find out the cause of the accident. We were on our homeward journey when the controls & two engines went out of order, & we had a fire in the nose. George & Doug managed [to] extinguish the fire, but we also had another one in the rear of the machine. We all fixed on our chutes, but we found out we were cut off from the escape hatches by fire, as the nose went on fire again. The aircraft blew up in mid-air, causing me to be blown out. Bill also was blown out of the turret, as he was getting out of it at the time. The German civillians[sic] told Bill & I that five bodies had been found near the wreckage—as proof they brought Ray Eberle's flying boot to us. I couldn't realise it for quite a time about the misfortune of the rest of the crew, as they were the finest crew I had ever known. We all had great faith in George—he was a first-class navigator, and a very good comrade & friend. Bill, George & I lived in the same room on the Squadron, & we got on together as though we had known each other for years. I was only with the crew four months, as engineers are the last members to join up before the start of operations. I was never

* Bill Baker was subsequently held as a prisoner of war at Stalag Luft III. In a 15 November 1944 letter to the International Red Cross's Central Agency for Prisoners of War, he gave this account of the crash: "The last contact I had with any of the crew was when the skipper gave the order to bale out. Just after, the aircraft exploded and consequently I cannot say what became of the crew. I have not seen or heard anything of the crew since becoming a prisoner."

told the name of the village where we were captured, but it is very close to Hameln, which is situated South-East of Hanover.

I have had no news of Bill Baker since the morning we were captured, as he went to hospital & subsequently to a different prison camp.*

George told me of his brother, & the trips in the car on a Saturday to Saskatoon. He also mentioned about the farm, & small incidents that had happened when he was younger in his work. George was very pleased when he found out I was younger than him, as I then took the title of being "the baby of the crew," although the average of the ages was about twenty-two.

I offer you my deepest sympathy in your great loss. I will always rem[em]ber them, as a finer set of friends I have yet to meet.

I will now close, & hope this finds you in perfect health.

> Yours sincerely,
> W. Morement

LETTER 116.

> Summerberry, Sask.
> September 5, 1945

Dear Sir,

In reply to your letter of Aug. 27th, my son R142247 Flt. Sgt. George McCowan King had no dependents[sic]. He voluntarily assigned thirty dollars per month to his mother, Mrs Agnes King, Summerberry, Sask.

> Yours truly,
> William King.

LETTER 117.

Ottawa, Canada
September 14, 1945

Mr. William King,
Summerberry, Sask.

Dear Mr. King:

We have your letter of September 5th, regarding War Service Gratuity on behalf of Flight Sergeant G. McC. King.

According to the regulations, the gratuity is payable, firstly to the dependents, and secondly, if there are no dependents, into the service estate of the personnel concerned. This is then distributed according to the Will.

Your letter is being used as an application, and you will be advised further as to your entitlement in the near future.

Yours truly,
S.
for T.K McDougall, Group Captain
for Chief of the Air Staff.

LETTER 118.

Ottawa, Ontario*
October 9th, 1945

Mr. William King,
Summerberry, Sask.

Dear Mr. King,

Your application for the war service gratuity in respect of the late Flight Sergeant George M. King has been reviewed.

* This is a form letter, with the date, greeting, names, and pronoun "she" typed in after the fact. It is not actually signed by the Air Commodore.

We note that you have intimated that no one was dependent at the date of death which, under normal conditions, would enable us to make payment into the deceased member's service estate.

However, since pay was assigned to Mrs. Agnes King at the time of the member's death, the receipt of which may indicate the possibility of dependency and since payment can only be made to the service estate where dependency did not exist, will you kindly arrange for that person to confirm to us that she was not dependent upon the deceased.

Upon receipt of this advice, we shall arrange for the gratuity to be paid into the deceased member's service estate for distribution in accordance with the terms of his will.

Since the advice requested will be of distinct assistance to us, an early reply will be appreciated.

The letter should be addressed to The Secretary, Department of National Defence for Air, Ottawa, (Attention: DAF/War Service Gratuity Section), and should quote the above file number.

Yours truly,
J. MacL. Murray.
Air Commodore
for Chief of the Air Staff

LETTER 119.

Summerberry, Sask.
October 21st, 1945*

Secretary
Department of National Defence for Air
Ottawa

Dear Sir,

My son, Flt. Sgt. George McCowan King R142247 had no dependents[sic]. The money assigned to me by him was for safe keeping until he got back. Hoping this explains what you want to know.

Yours truly,
Agnes King.

LETTER 120.

Ottawa, Ontario*
October 31st, 1945

Mr. William King,
Summerberry, Sask.

Dear Sir,

Your application for the war service gratuity in respect of the late Flight Sergeant George M. King has been reviewed by the authorities responsible for determining entitlement.

It is advised that payment will be made into his service estate for distribution to the person or persons named as beneficiaries under his will, or, in the absence of a will, to the person or persons entitled by law to receive the gratuity.

Distribution may be expected within the reasonably near future.

* This letter is written on the back of the 9 October letter from the Air Commodore.

* This is a form letter not actually signed by the Air Commodore.

However, in those cases where the estate has not yet been settled, payment will be delayed awaiting the final disposition of all service assets.

Any further enquiries should be directed to the Estates Branch, 308 Sparks Street, Ottawa, Ontario, (Attention: War Service Gratuity Section).

Yours truly,
J. Macl. Murray
Air Commodore
for Chief of the Air Staff

LETTER 121.

Ottawa, Canada
September 16, 1946

Mr. William King,
Summerberry, Saskatchewan

Dear Mr. King:

It is a privilege to have the opportunity of sending you the Operational Wings and Certificate in recognition of the gallant services rendered by your son, Flight Sergeant G.M. King.

I realise there is little which may be said or done to lessen your sorrow, but it is my hope that these "Wings," indicative of operations against the enemy, will be a treasured memento of a young life offered on the altar of freedom in defence of his Home and Country.

Yours very sincerely,
W.A. Dicks, G/C
R.C.A.F. Records Officer

Encl.

LETTER 122.

R.C.A.F. Casualty Officer
For Chief of the Air Staff
Royal Canadian Air Force
Ottawa, Ontario
January 28th, 1947

Mr. W. King
Summerberry, Saskatchewan

Dear Mr. King,

Information has been received from the Authorities Overseas regarding your son, Flight Sergeant George McCowan King.

Your son's aircraft crashed at Pohle, 15 miles South West of Hanover, Germany. Sergeant Morement and Warrant Officer Baker were captured, the remainder of the crew losing their lives. They were laid to rest in the nearby Lauenau Protestant Cemetery in a Comrades Grave by the Germans. Your son and his crew will be reinterred in a permanent military cemetery and at this time an attempt will be made to effect individual identification of the crew.

You will be advised the results of this investigation immediately [as soon as] they are available at these Headquarters.

British Military Cemeteries have been located at a number of points in Germany, and all Royal Canadian Air Force personnel buried in Germany will be moved to these cemeteries, where the graves will be supported and sustained by the Dominion of Canada and entrusted to the Imperial War Graves Commission for reverent and perpetual care and the erection of a headstone over each grave. The task of preparing and erecting these headstones will naturally take considerable time. It is not necessary to write to the Imperial War Graves Commission, as you will be contacted by them before the stone is prepared.

May I again, at this time, extend my sincere sympathy at the loss of your son.

Yours sincerely,
[signature illegible]
R.C.A.F. Casualty Officer
for Chief of the Air Staff

LETTER 123.

R.C.A.F. Casualty Officer
For Chief of the Air Staff
Royal Canadian Air Force
Ottawa, Ontario
July 9th, 1947

Dear Mr. King,

It is with regret that I again refer to the loss of your son, Flight Sergeant George McCowan King, but we have received a report from our Overseas Headquarters which states that your son has now been re-interred in the Hannover (Limmer) British Military Cemetery. He has been buried collectively with two other members of his crew and their places have been registered as Graves No. 1-3, Row H, Plot 2. This cemetery is located 3 1/2 miles west of the centre of Hannover in Germany.

This is a Permanent British Military Cemetery in Germany and will be turned over shortly to the Imperial War Graves Commission (of which Canada is a member), who are responsible for the reverent and perpetual care of the resting places of our Fallen. The cemeteries will be beautified by landscaping and the planting of shrubs and flowers, and a headstone will be erected at each grave. Unhappily, there are great numbers of these headstones to be erected, and it will quite naturally take considerable time. It is not necessary to write to the Imperial War Graves Commission, as you will be contacted by them before the stone is prepared.

May I again offer you my most sincere sympathy in the loss of your gallant son.

Yours sincerely,
[signature illegible]
R.C.A.F. Casualty Officer,
for Chief of the Air Staff

LETTER 124.

W.A. Dicks
Wing Commander
For Chief of the Air Staff
Royal Canadian Air Force
Ottawa, Ontario
February 4th, 1948

Mr W. King,
Summerberry, Sask.
Re: G.M. King (R.142247)

The enclosed log book which is part of the service estate of the above named is passed herewith for your retention.

Yours truly,
W.A. Dicks
Wing Commander,
for Chief of the Air Staff

The graves of the aircrew of Stirling Mk. III EF 139, Hanover Military Cemetery. Left to right, Norman Spencer, George King, Douglas Wylie, Harold Hicks, and Raymond Eberle.

Excerpt from the flight log book of F/S G.M. King

Date	Duty	Remarks
Aug. 24/43	Navigator	Operation. Mining Frisians.
Aug. 25/43	Navigator	Operation. Mining Deordas.
Aug. 27/43	Navigator	Operation. Nuremburg[sic]. Returned with port inner engine V/S. feathered.
Aug. 30/43	Navigator	Operation. Munchen. Gladbach[sic]. Rheydt.
Aug. 31/43	Navigator	Operation. Berlin.
Sept. 2/43	Navigator	Fighter Affiliation.
Sept. 4/43	Navigator	Bombing Detail.
Sept. 4/43	Navigator	Fighter Affiliation.
Sept. 5/43	Navigator	Operations.
Sept. 7/43	Navigator	Fighter Affiliation.
Sept. 15/43	Navigator	Operations.
Sept. 16/43	Navigator	Operations.
Sept. 19/43	Navigator	Air Test.
Sept. 20/43	Navigator	Formation Flying and Air Firing.
Sept. 22/43	Navigator	Missing.

Minister of Natural Res...

Mr. James King,
Box 121,
NORTH PORTAL, Saskatchewan.

Dear Mr. King:

    I was indeed pleased to receive your letter advising that you are the brother of F/S George M. King after whom "King Creek" has been named.

    "King Creek" is situated approximately forty miles east of Fond du Lac and is two and three quarter miles long.

    "King Creek" as indicated on the attached map has been officially adopted as a Canadian map and place name and will appear on future revised maps of the Wiley Lake area of Saskatchewan.

    I trust the naming of the feature in memory of your valiant brother will be of some comfort to you and the members of your family.

    I am today writing a letter to your mother and enclosing a map indicating "King Creek".

                      Sincerely yours,

                      A. G. Kuziak.

LETTER 125.

Ottawa, Canada
May 6th, 1949

Mr. W. King,
Summerberry, Saskatchewan

Dear Mr. King,

Please find enclosed a photograph which has been received from Overseas, of the grave of your son, Flight Sergeant George McCowan King.

Cemeteries are being handed over progressively to the Imperial War Graves Commission, of which Canada is a member, who are entrusted with the perpetual maintenance of the resting places of all our Fallen, and who will beautify the graves and surroundings, and erect a permanent headstone at each grave.

It is not necessary for you to contact the Commission. Any discrepancy as to rank, etc., which may appear on the temporary cross shown in the enclosed photograph, will appear correctly on the permanent headstone.*

Yours sincerely,
[signature illegible]
for (J.G. Stephenson)
Group Captain,
for Chief of the Air Staff

Encl. 2

The temporary cross on George's grave at Hannover Military Cemetery, 1949.

* Ironically, despite the statement that the name will appear correctly on the permanent headstone, on the Canadian Virtual War Memorial at www.vac-acc.gc.ca, George's name appears as "George McGowan King." I have not yet visited George's grave in Europe, and so I do not know if his name is registered correctly there.

LETTER 126.

Ottawa, Ontario
June 2nd, 1951*

Mr. W. King,
Summerberry, Saskatchewan

Dear Mr. King,

It is with reluctance that I must again refer to the loss of your son, Flight Sergeant George McCowan King. A communication has, however, been received from the Graves Registration Service which states that, as a result of an examination of the exhumation reports of Graves 1, 2, and 3 in Row H, Plot 2, in Hannover (Limmer) British Military Cemetery in which your son and two other members of his crew are buried collectively, sufficient information has been obtained to warrant registering these graves as individual graves. Grave No. 2 is now registered in the name of your son.

May I take this opportunity to again extend my sincere sympathy.

Yours sincerely,
[signature illegible]
for (W.R. Gunn) Wing Commander
R.C.A.F. Casualties Officer,
for Chief of the Air Staff

LETTER 127.

Imperial War Graves Commission
Wooburn House
Wooburn Place
High Wycombe
Buckinghamshire, England
December 9th, 1953

The Imperial War Graves Commission have the honour to inform you that the task of erecting the permanent memorials on war graves all over the world is nearing completion.

Among the memorials already erected are those on war graves in Hanover War Cemetery, Germany.*

Although you may already know this, it is thought that you would wish to have this official notification.

LETTER 128.

Minister of Natural Resources
Province of Saskatchewan
Govt. Admin. Building
Regina, Saskatchewan
May 29th, 1961

Mr. James King,
North Portal, Saskatchewan.

Dear Mr. King,

I was indeed pleased to receive your letter advising that you are the brother of F/S George M. King after whom "King Creek" has been named.

"King Creek" is situated approximately forty miles east of Fond du Lac and is two and three quarter miles long.† "King Creek" as

* The name of the cemetery was typed after the fact onto this form letter.

Detail from the map sent to George's mother.

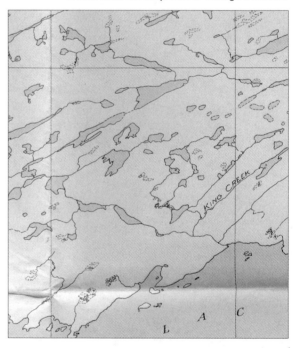

† King Creek is located at 59° 18'N, 106° 11'W, just south of the Saskatchewan/Northwest Territories border. See an aerial photo of King Creek on the back cover of this book.

indicated on the attached map has been officially adopted as a Canadian map and place name and will appear on future revised maps of the Wiley Lake area of Saskatchewan.

I trust the naming of the feature in memory of your valiant brother will be of some comfort to you and the members of your family.

I am today writing a letter to your mother and enclosing a map indicating "King Creek."

Sincerely yours,
A.G. Kuziak.

LETTER 129.

James King
Box 121
North Portal, Sask.
August 20, 1961

Mr. A.G. Kuziak,
Minister of Natural Resources,
Government Administration Building,
Regina, Saskatchewan.

Dear Mr. Kuziak:

Please accept my apologies for not writing to you sooner.

My mother, Mrs. Agnes King of Grenfell, Saskatchewan, asked me to send you a biographical sketch of my brother, F/S George M. King, after whom "King Creek" has been named.

George M. King was born on April 19, 1922, at Summerberry, Saskatchewan. He received his education at Summerberry and joined the R.C.A.F. in the fall of 1941. He trained at Brandon and Regina and graduated as a navigator at Pearce, Alberta, in October 1942. Overseas he was attached to #218 "Gold Coast" sqdn. of the R.A.F. at

King's Lynn, Norfolk. He was killed with four other members of his crew over Hanover, Germany, on September 22, 1943.

The naming of "King Creek" after my brother has given a great deal of comfort to my mother. On her behalf and also for myself, I would like to thank you very much for your interest and also for the maps which you so kindly sent.

I hope sometime to take a trip into the northern part of the province and possibly be able to go to see "King Creek."

Yours truly,
James King.

LETTER 130.

The Sergeant-at-Arms
House of Commons
Ottawa, Ontario
November 5th, 1997

Dear Mr. King,

On behalf of the Speaker of the House of Commons, the Honourable Gilbert Parent, I am pleased to enclose a photocopy of page 177 from the Book of Remembrance of the Second World War.

Inscribed on this page is the name of Flight Sergeant George McCowan King, Royal Canadian Air Force. A grateful nation recognizes his sacrifice every year on April 12th, when this page is displayed for public viewing in the Chapel of the Parliament of Canada.

In the same sense of gratitude, this page is sent to you with the sincere hope it will remain a source of pride for your family.

Yours sincerely,
M.G. Cloutier
Major-General

Below, George King's page from the Book of Remembrance. George's name is the tenth name in the second column.

Note on Sources

The bulk of the material contained in the main body of this book—letters, a newspaper article, diary entries, and log book entries—comes from a collection of papers that I inherited from my father. Other letters, as well as supplementary information in the introduction, are taken from George McCowan King's military file, National Archives of Canada Military Personnel File RG 24, Volume 00-27905. Much of the information in footnotes about people mentioned in the letters comes from memory, since my father was always eager to reminisce about his youth in the Summerberry district. I also gained information about references in the letters by consulting with numerous people currently living in the Summerberry district. When I refer either directly or indirectly to textual sources, I have footnoted the references and included the sources under Works Cited.

I recommend several other texts to the reader who wishes to learn more about RCAF life during the Second World War. Larry Milberry and Hugh Halliday's *The Royal Canadian Air Force at War: 1939-1945* (Toronto: CANAV Books, 1990) is a thorough study of all aspects of the RCAF in wartime. Sydney F. Wise's *The Crucible of War: 1939-1945* (Toronto: University of Toronto in co-operation with the Department of National Defence, c.1980), the third volume of *The Official History of the Royal Canadian Air Force*, is an in-depth study of Bomber Command operations overseas. *A Thousand Shall Fall* (Stittsville, ON: Canada's Wings, 1979) by Murray Peden is an excellent personal account of RCAF training and operations in Stirling bombers. *Terror in the Starboard Seat* (Don Mills, ON: General Publishing, 1980) by Dave McIntosh is a detailed account of an R.C.A.F. navigator's life on operations. And C.P. Stacey and Barbara Wilson's *The Half-Million: The Canadians in Britain, 1939-1946* (Toronto: University of Toronto Press, c. 1987) describes in an entertaining fashion the wartime interaction between RCAF personnel and British civilians. For more information about the Geographic Names program, and for stories about and a comprehensive listing of Saskatchewan's World War II casualties, see Doug Chisholm's *Their Names Live On: Remembering Saskatchewan's Fallen in World War II* (Regina: Canadian Plains Research Center, 2001).

Works Cited

Bridging the Past: Wolseley and District, 1880-1980. Wolseley, Sask.: Wolseley and District History Book Committee, 1981.

Dunmore, Spencer. *Wings for Victory: The Remarkable Story of the British Commonwealth Air Training Plan in Canada.* Toronto: McClelland and Stewart, 1994.

— and William Carter. *Reap the Whirlwind: The Untold Story of 6 Group, Canada's Bomber Force of World War II.* Toronto: McClelland and Stewart, 1991.

Ellis, Chris, ed. *World War II: A Visual Encyclopedia.* London: PRC Publishing Ltd., 1999.

English, Allan D. *The Cream of the Crop: Canadian Aircrew, 1939-1945.* Montreal: McGill-Queen's UP, 1996.

Galbraith, Iva W. and Iris Smith, eds. *Centennial Tribute: The Story of Broadview and Area.* Broadview, Sask.: Broadview Pioneer History Society, 1982.

Gunston, Bill. *The Illustrated Directory of Fighting Aircraft of World War II.* London: Salamander Books Limited, 1988.

Harris, Sir Arthur. *Bomber Offensive.* London: Collins, 1947.

McCaffery, Dan. *Battlefields in the Air: Canadians in the Allied Bomber Command.* Toronto: J. Lorimer and Co., 1995.

Middlebrook, Martin, and Chris Everitt. *Bomber Command War Diaries: An Operational Reference Book, 1939-1945.* Harmondsworth: Viking, 1985.

Moyes, Philip J.R. *Bomber Squadrons of the R.A.F. and Their Aircraft.* London: MacDonald and James, 1964.

Neagle, Anna. *Anna Neagle Says "There's Always Tomorrow": An Autobiography.* London: W.H. Allen, 1974.

Ward, Norman and David Smith. *Jimmy Gardiner: Relentless Liberal.* Toronto: University of Toronto Press, 1990.

Webster, Sir Charles and Noble Frankland. *The Strategic Air Offensive Against Germany, 1939-1945.* London: Her Majesty's Stationery Office, 1961. vol. 2.

Zinkhan, John. "Aircrew Training." *The Grenfell Sun* 104.42 (7 November 2000): B10.